A Western Horseman Book

STARTING COLTS

By Mike Kevil

With Pat Close

Photographs by Darrell Arnold

STARTING COLTS

Published by
Western Horseman Inc.

3850 North Nevada Ave.
Box 7980
Colorado Springs, CO 80933-7980

Design, Typography, and Production
Western Horseman
Colorado Springs, Colorado

Printing
Publisher's Press
Salt Lake City, Utah

Nineteenth Printing: October 2000

ISBN 0-911647-21-X

DEDICATION

I am thankful to so many people for so many things.
However, at the top of the list are, without a doubt, my parents,
Walter and Georgia Ruesga, who live in Chino, California.
Much of what they instilled in me—manners, patience,
respect, etc.—I try to instill in the horses I ride.
I'd also like to thank all the people from whom I have learned, for
without them, this book would be a lot thinner. I have listed some
of them under my "Acknowledgments." This book was written
with all my gratitude to them.
I would also like to dedicate this book to all the riders and trainers
who crave knowledge as much as I do.

Mike Kevil

MIKE KEVIL

PREFACE

Many readers skip over sections of a book to get to the part that interests them the most. Take a book on how to fly, for example. The most exciting part will be the chapter detailing your first flight at the controls. But if that's the only chapter you read, strap on a parachute 'cause you'll get into serious trouble. Before you ever climb into the cockpit, there's much to be learned.

It's the same way with horse training. Everyone wants a horse that can make beautiful lead changes and sensational stops. But there is a lot a horse must learn before he can do advanced maneuvers.

I bring this up because I have written this book in an orderly fashion that gives you the knowledge to go from one step to the next. There is a reason for each step: to build a foundation for the next . . . so there will be consistent progression in your training program. Each new step overlaps the previous one so you are building on what the horse has already learned. If you skip a step or two, you are cheating your horse, and at some point it will show up. He will not be as well-rounded and solid a horse as if you had taken the proper time.

The intent of this book is to serve as a guide to anyone who wants to break his or her own horse, regardless of experience. I have not meant to talk down to the good hands, or over the heads of beginners; I have simply said what I think needs to be said on this subject. I hope it will prove equally helpful to the novice as well as the experienced.

I emphasize going slowly and taking plenty of time with a colt. Don't be concerned if you are not progressing as fast with your colt as you think you should be—or as fast as your friend is with his colt. He might have more experience than you, and is working with a gentle, easygoing colt, whereas yours might be a little more difficult and need more time.

It's possible to be riding a colt within an hour. But there is a greater risk of something bad happening when you get on your colt too soon. The longer you work with him from the ground, the more control you can put on him. That will build your confidence because you know that when you finally step on, it's very likely nothing will happen. If something does go wrong, you'll be okay because you can quickly bring the colt back under control. So take your time. There's no rule that says you must ride your colt on the first day, or even within the first week.

Stay within your abilities. For example, I can get on almost any colt the first day and walk, trot, and lope him with no problems because I have years of experience in dealing with all kinds of colts. But if a novice were to try it, chances are he might get into a storm. This ties in with taking your time and teaching this colt all the things he needs to know before you advance with him. This will also give you the control you need in any situation.

I believe an improvement can be made in any horse, and I will encourage and help any rider willing to try. The question is: Is it feasible for you—worth your time, effort, and money? It may be simpler to just get another horse that fits you better. After all, we trade our cars and trucks in for something different so they can meet the needs we have at the time. Why not a horse?

If you are wanting a challenge, there are plenty of horses out there that are in need of work. But if you need a first-time horse for your children, it is a mistake to get a young or inexperienced horse so that they can "learn together." Instead, get a proven, older horse that is known to be safe. In other words, get a horse that fits your needs.

Be a realist. By this I mean there are plenty of young horses that are rank, ill-mannered, stubborn, have a strong tendency to buck, or all of the above. With such a colt, a novice should swallow his pride and realize that discretion is much the better part of valor. Let someone experienced put at least the first 30 days on this type of colt.

Remember that safety is always first. Never allow yourself to get in a situation or position where you might get hurt. For example: riding with an old, worn-out cinch, and thinking, "It's lasted this long; it's good for one more ride." The time to replace it is before it breaks. If you are not sure about something, don't use it, or don't do it.

Always remember to use common sense when working with or around horses. Ask yourself, "Am I liable to get hurt doing this?" And second, "Is my horse liable to get hurt if I do this?" If you can answer no to both questions, only then should you proceed.

Also remember that on any given day, your mood will have a direct influence on your training. A good mood won't give you or your horse any more talent or smarts, but it will let you live up to your potential.

The last thing I want to tell you is to have fun. If you are not enjoying yourself or looking forward to the training, then leave it to someone else.

—Mike Kevil

PHILOSOPHY

If someone were to ask you to write down how you train a horse, you would think that's impossible; it would take a book to explain it. However, you could answer it correctly with two simple words: *stimulus* and *response.* There is a little more to it than that, but that's training in a nutshell.

You apply a stimulus until you get the desired response, then you stop the stimulus.

For example, if you are teaching a colt to lead, you pull lightly on the lead rope. This puts pressure on the crownpiece of the halter behind the ears. The colt might do many things trying to get away from this pressure, but not until he takes a step forward—the desired response—do you relieve the pressure. By repeating this over and over, the colt will stop trying everything else and simply step forward. After learning this, he will begin to respond faster and faster. You have now created a learned behavior in this horse.

Knowing how a horse learns is a big part of training, but not all of it. Lots of people are aware of this theory, but everybody applies it just a little differently. The more quietly you can teach a horse something, the better he'll accept and remember it.

We are many levels above horses in the ability to think. But if we were put under

the same conditions some horses are under, we would react in much the same way. The reason for this, I think, is because under pressure we don't think; we react. If our reaction reduces the pressure, then we made the right choice. If, however, the pressure is not reduced, or if it is increased, our instinct is to react more strongly.

In my training, I want to increase the chances of a horse making the correct decision. The best way I know to do this is to teach so the horse learns in a soft, non-traumatic way. He will then accept it and do it willingly thereafter. Then, if this horse is ever put under pressure, chances are he will react in the way I want him to. That was how he reacted the first time, the last time—every time. Therefore, his automatic reflex kicks in and he does it my way.

If a training session is going badly—the horse cannot comprehend what I want—I will review something simple, that he understands, rather than trying to make him do something more difficult. By trying to progress too fast, you can get into a fight and cause more problems. I have seen too many people having to take time to fix problems they caused. They take three steps forward and four back. I would rather take one step at a time, with each step being a solid one. It may be slower, but each step will be in the right direction. At the very least, I won't take a step at all. Insisting on that one step when it won't happen is what will set you back the four steps.

Throughout this book I have expressed most of my philosophy. Here are some of the most important points.

1/ Go slowly. (Tired of hearing that yet?)

2/ Be patient.

3/ Practice your feel and timing on a horse constantly.

4/ Prepare yourself and your horse for everything you do.

5/ If the horse seems confused, ask for something more simple. Make sure he understands.

6/ When asking for more, make sure it's just a little more.

7/ Don't let time or other people pressure you into hurrying. Taking an extra 30 days now will seem like nothing when this horse is 8 years old.

8/ Be a good detective. If your horse is having a problem, try to determine exactly what's causing it before you start "fixing" him.

9/ If you want your horse to stop doing something, use negative reinforcement. Example: He is chewing the fence. You paint it with something that tastes bad. He stops because it is no longer enjoyable.

10/ If you want a horse to continue do-ing something, use positive reinforcement. Example: Your horse is hard to catch. Bait him with a little grain and scratch him when he's caught, and he will be easier to catch next time. The horse found some-thing good in being caught and will look forward to it.

There are some people with more pa-tience than others. There are some who are very athletic with quick reflexes and excellent timing. Other people may be more compassionate to horses. Some peo-ple are better trainers because they know when to quit working a horse. One per-son's strength may be another's weakness. But I believe we can all train horses.

When I see a person doing something on a horse, I tell myself, "I can do that." I *can*, and so can you. All I need to know is *how* it's done; then I'll practice it until I can do it, too. Maybe I won't be the best in the world at it, but I can learn to be good. There are times when I have to work twice as hard as someone else to be as good as they are. But when I finally get as good, I think it makes me twice as happy.

If somebody's better than you, maybe he (or she) has just worked harder. Lots of hard work can make up for a lack of tal-ent. I believe anybody can do what I'm doing. You just need the know-how, and then you must practice. This book con-tains the know-how—the rest is up to you.

ACKNOWLEDGMENTS

I have learned something from everyone for whom I have worked, and every place I have worked—from dude strings to the racetracks to the show ring. Specifically, I would like to mention:

Keith Hagler. He taught me how to work around colts without getting killed. It might have been the school of hard knocks, but the lessons were all worth it. He never told me in these words, but I learned *nothing is impossible,* and *not knowing how to do something doesn't mean you can't try.* Without his schooling, I wouldn't have been hired by the rest of these men.

Shorty Freeman. He taught me to be patient and that doing less with a horse can sometimes result in getting more done.

Matlock Rose. Many people tend to imitate him, but nobody can. He could often get more out of a horse than anybody else could. An exceptional man with many talents.

Gene LaCroix. This man has better feel and timing than anyone else I know. He knocked a lot of rough edges off me. He taught me how to make a horse light, but more important, how to make a horse soft. The basic lessons I learned at Lasma Arabians are the foundation of my training today.

Kenny Kimball. From him I learned about the racetrack game, and the importance of conditioning and of good feet and legs.

Al Dunning. He gave me the opportunity to ride a lot of good horses, and from him I really learned how to stop a horse.

Don Dodge. A horseman's horseman. I can't tell you all that I learned from Don because I am still learning. He is a very intelligent man who is well read and knows of what he speaks. He instilled in me the significance of the basics and the importance of a solid foundation. But that's only the tip of the iceberg. From Don I've learned a lot about legs, conditioning, feeding, medications, race horses, jumping horses, cutting, reining, and on and on. The icing on the cake is all the old stories Don tells.

George Kevil. My brother has worked many places and always comes up with something new or a different twist on something old. He has always been a big help to me. Besides being a good cowman, he is also a good hand with a horse and can pack, hunt, and trap, and braid gear better than most people. He has lots of hidden talents that will surface one day.

I would also like to thank all the folks at *Western Horseman* for their help with this book.

Finally, a special thanks to Molly Enright and Diane Kallal for their help . . . I couldn't have done it without them.

CONTENTS

1 ROUND PEN & FACILITIES

The safest place for starting a young horse is in a round pen.

HORSE OWNERS all have different facilities with which to work. On a ranch you might have a large set of corrals, or maybe just a few small holding pens—plus big pastures. In town, you might have anything from a breaking pen and large arena to the street in front of your house.

I've had to start colts with all kinds of facilities (or the lack of). If you really want to do it, you make do with what you have. Sometimes you have to use your imagination and be inventive to stay out of trouble, but anything is possible.

However, the safest place for starting a young horse is in a round pen. It's safest for the horse, and safest for you.

I have a round pen, built out of stout posts and lumber, that measures 50 feet in diameter. The sides are 7 feet high, and are solid up to 4 feet and covered with rubber

My round pen is 50 feet in diameter with a 7-foot fence. The fence is solid up to about 4 feet, and then has spacing between the boards for better air circulation. The inside of the fence has rubber matting on the bottom portion to save wear and tear on the boards and horses.

The posts are power-line poles, 12 feet long, set 4 feet into the ground, and angled out slightly to allow more clearance for a rider's knees. The planks are rough 2 by 12s and 2 by 10s, bolted to the posts.

matting. There's spacing between the top boards, which allows for ventilation in the Arizona heat. A completely solid side discourages real bad horses from trying to jump out, and also holds the attention of the horse you are working with, because he can't see out.

However, I don't mind a fence that a horse can see through. First of all, not many horses could jump a 7-foot fence, and I don't put enough pressure on my horses to make them try. I think it's good they can see what's going on outside the round pen. They learn to pay attention to me despite outside distractions.

I have had horses that were doing good in a round pen, but when I took them outside, it was like a whole new world to them. They had trouble listening to me because of all the things going on that they had never seen before.

But I do like the walls solid up to 3 or 4 feet from the bottom. This will keep the horse's legs from going through the fence if he gets a little wild. And when you are riding, it will keep your toes from being caught on a post and twisted backwards.

I cover the bottom portion of the sides with rubber matting. It prevents the lumber from being worn or broken as quickly. And because it has a smooth surface, it helps prevent injury if you or the horse rub or bang up against it.

I like a 12-foot gate. Colts will ride or lead easier through a wider opening than a

I used a Powder River 12-foot pipe gate, and wired ¾-inch exterior plywood to it. The 12-foot width allows me to drive a tractor into the pen to work up the ground.

narrow one. I can also back a trailer into the pen for loading or unloading, and can take a tractor in to work up the ground. If a 12-foot gate is balanced properly, it won't be any harder to open than a small one.

I like the ground to be soft, but not deep. Hard ground is bad for your horse's

11

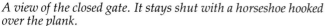

A view of the closed gate. It stays shut with a horseshoe hooked over the plank.

Just outside of the gate is this equipment rack—built of horseshoes welded to a strip of flat iron.

feet and legs, and if it gets wet, it's too slippery. Deep ground puts too much strain on a young horse's legs, and can cause any horse to stumble. Wet or slick ground is the worst kind. Not only can a horse fall, but the constant slipping puts a strain on him. He could end up sore or permanently injured from steady work on this kind of ground.

I also like a good, stout post for tying. It can be part of the round-pen fence, as mine is, or you can set a post just outside of the fence. This would be a good solution, for example, if your round pen is built of portable pipe panels.

Some people use a snubbing post in the middle of the pen, and it works good for them. Personally, it gets in my way, especially when I'm on the ground longeing. If I tie up to it, the horse might walk around and 'round it until he has snubbed his nose right up to the post, causing him to fight it.

If I'm riding in the round pen, I worry about a colt or horse taking me too close to the post and banging my knees. A

horse throwing a fit could also crash into it and get hurt.

I could work around these problems, but using a post in the fence, or just outside the fence, eliminates them.

Once I start to ride my horses outside the breaking pen, I prefer to ride somewhere away from fences, such as in a large field or pasture or out on the desert. But when I need to ride in an arena, I like a large one—preferably one that measures about 300 by 150 feet. I like it large for the same reason I like to ride outside: In a small arena, fences influence the way a horse will travel.

This is why I take a horse out of the breaking pen and into a larger area as soon as I have control of him. Some horses get so used to loping in a 50-foot pen that when you put them in a larger area, they'll still lope 50-foot circles. They don't know how to line out and go somewhere.

Other horses feel secure only when next to a fence because they have always been loped next to one. They don't feel

12

Although I have two enclosed center-aisle barns, with a total of 18 stalls, I also have this barn, which is ideal for our climate. All of the pens are under roof (galvanized metal) and are bedded in shavings. Each pen measures about 12 by 12 feet, has an automatic waterer, and a feeder that holds hay and grain. The pipe is 1½ inches in diameter, and the sides of each pen are 5 feet high. There are several fluorescent lights over the 12-foot aisleway. Just to the left, in this photo, is a hay storage area.

comfortable unless they stay alongside the fence in an arena. A young colt, or any horse, will look ahead to where he's loping, see a corner coming up, and turn before you ask him. No sooner does he turn than he sees the next corner coming up, so he turns again. Next thing you know, he's cutting all the corners.

Then when you're loping, you're having to pull on the outside rein to make a larger circle. This is a contradiction to the way we want to train the horse, which is to pull on the left rein when we want to go left, and right rein when we want to go right.

In short, fences can create problems, giving the horse a false sense of security, and also resulting in a horse that leans into or out of his circles. When riding in a larger area, or out in the open, the barriers are farther apart and less likely to influence the horse.

But for safety's sake, always ride in a confined area until you have sufficient control.

Bill Bouwhivs rinses off a horse on the wash rack. The concrete slab was poured at a slight angle to facilitate drainage.

13

2 EQUIPMENT

I make my own lead ropes out of old nylon lariat ropes.

WHEN YOU are working with horses, you absolutely need *good* equipment, because poor equipment can easily break and get you or the horse hurt. Buying good equipment usually means paying a bigger price, but always remember that you get what you pay for.

Correct fit is something else to keep in mind. Equipment that does not fit properly can irritate or injure a horse.

Halters

There are a variety on the market today, but we are primarily interested in halters for everyday use. Most of these are made of nylon webbing, although some are made of leather or synthetic rope. Nylon is popular because it's sturdy and durable, and doesn't need the maintenance that leather halters do. Leather halters, as well as some of the cheaper rope halters, won't hold up under a lot of pressure, and might break if a horse pulls back when tied.

Something else that can break is the hardware—rings and buckles—used on halters. If they are made of cheap pot metal, they will break easily, even though the webbing of the halter never breaks. When buying a halter, pay attention to the hardware—it should be made of stainless steel or brass.

The same is true with a lead rope. The rope itself can be stout enough to tie up the *Queen Mary,* but if it has a cheap snap, it's apt to break. You never want your lead rope—or halter—to break; not only will the horse get loose, he's likely to get hurt. He could flip over backwards when

the rope or halter breaks, or run into a fence, across a highway, etc.

Cotton lead ropes are popular because they are soft on your hands, but they are not as durable as lead ropes made of synthetic material, such as nylon. I make my own lead ropes. I take an old nylon lariat rope, unravel it, and rebraid it. I double it so it's larger in circumference and therefore easier to handle than a regular nylon lariat.

I also braid a loop and a button at one end that I can use for attaching the rope to the halter. That way, I eliminate having a snap that might break. Some people braid their lead rope right into the halter ring,

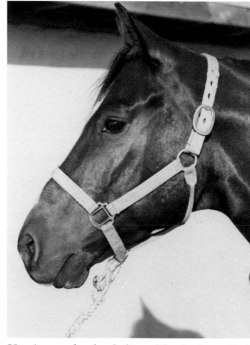

Here's a good nylon halter with a lead rope that I braided from a nylon lariat rope.

In my lead ropes I braid a loop and button at one end for attaching to the halter. This eliminates use of a snap that might break.

and that's okay—but if you ever want to remove it, you've got to cut it off.

If you buy a lead rope, get one that's stout and has a big, heavy-duty snap. Get it stouter than what you'll actually need, instead of just barely good enough.

Bridles

I want a bridle that's going to stay on my horse, especially if he's a colt I'm just breaking. That's why I like a throatlatch and browband on all my bridles, instead of a single earpiece. One time I had a one-ear bridle on a colt who bogged his head and actually bucked the bridle off. That would never have happened if the bridle had had a throatlatch.

It's also easy for a horse to accidentally (or intentionally) rub a one-ear bridle off while he's scratching his head on a post.

I like my bridles to be made out of good leather, ¾ to 1 inch wide, with sturdy buckles and other hardware.

Reins

I like leather reins that have a good feel to them, and that are about ½ to ⅝ inch wide and 7 feet long. I like long reins—not necessarily so I can whack a horse down the hind legs, but so I can give him plenty of slack and still have enough rein for me to hold. However, I start a lot of cutting horse prospects that are on the small side, and 7-foot reins are too long for them; the ends will drag on the ground. So I do have some shorter reins.

One thing I don't like are snaps for attaching the reins to the bit. These snaps bounce and clank against the metal of the bit, which can desensitize the horse's mouth just a little bit.

There are several ways of tying the reins to the bit, including lacing them; it really doesn't matter which method you use as long as the reins are securely tied. Some people use the thin leather that's doubled through the reins, and that's okay, but you need to watch them. Because those strips are small, they are more apt to break from the effects of sweat, saliva, and water.

Bits and Hackamores

Both hackamores and snaffle bits are fine for starting colts. Which to use depends partly on your personal preference and your skill in using them. However, I start all my colts in a snaffle because I feel that it gives me more control than a hackamore does, and in training, control is the key thing we want. (When I say hackamore, I am referring to one with a bosal—not a mechanical hackamore or hackamore bit.)

I use a regular snaffle with a smooth, sweet-iron mouthpiece that has copper inlay on the tongue side. The copper creates more saliva, which helps keep the mouth moist and therefore more responsive to the bit.

I start all my colts in a snaffle because I feel that it gives me more control than a hackamore does.

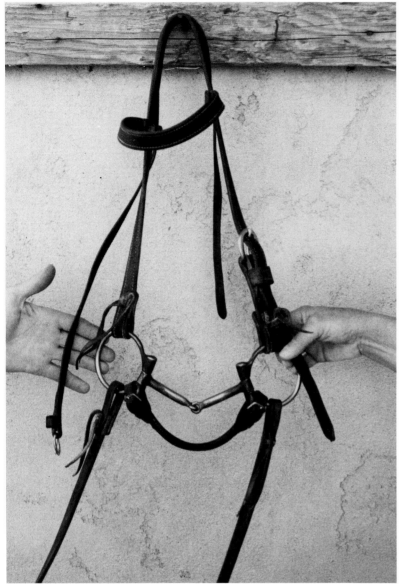

I like headstalls with a browband and throatlatch. I have them made out of 1-inch, double-stitched leather. The cheekpiece is extra long because I ride so many horses—including some with extra-long heads. This also shows the snaffle I use in starting colts; it's a Don Dodge snaffle made by Greg Darnall.

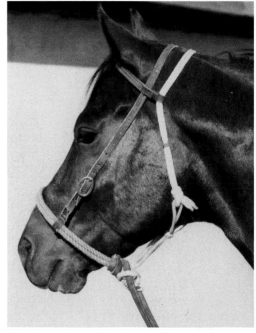

Here's one type of hackamore I'll sometimes use. This one was made by my brother, George Kevil. The bosal is made of lariat rope doubled to make it easier on the nose.

On a green colt that is just learning what a bit is, I would *never* use something like a twisted-wire snaffle, as it is too severe.

Snaffles come in various widths, and you should use the appropriate width for your colt. The standard width is 5 inches, however, and that will fit most horses.

There are a lot of times when I will switch to a hackamore just to get out of a colt's mouth for a while, and to let him relax. Because a hackamore applies different pressure, sometimes I can get things done on a colt that I couldn't with a snaffle. But overall, the snaffle is the best bit for most people to use.

The average person won't have the right kind of hackamore for a colt, and may not know how to use a hackamore properly. A hackamore doesn't offer the same control that a bit does. Also, if the hackamore is not used properly, the horse has a tendency to lean on the bosal, which makes a person pull on it more. This makes the colt get heavier and heavier—when we want him to be getting lighter and lighter.

16

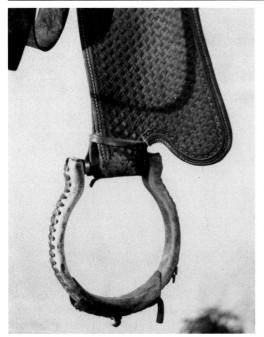

For breaking colts, I like oxbow stirrups because it's easier to keep my feet in them if I get into a storm. This is a metal oxbow covered with rawhide.

Saddles

For breaking horses, I prefer a lighter saddle than I normally use. That's because I sometimes have to lift the saddle onto a colt with one hand, and because colts that I break are generally on the smaller side. So a lightweight saddle is for my ease as well as theirs. But if a person has only one saddle and is going to be breaking only one or two colts a year, he's not going to go out and buy a special saddle. He can get along just fine using what he has.

If the saddle has a little bit more swell to it, and a little higher cantle, that would help you stay aboard if the colt were to jump around a little bit. But we are going to outline a program that will minimize his bucking, and that will give you good control when you do get on him the first time.

The most important thing in a saddle is a proper fit for both you and the horse. If it's not comfortable for you, you won't have much fun riding. It could also cause you to sit a little differently, distributing your weight incorrectly and, as a result, perhaps sore the horse's back.

For breaking colts and riding cutting horses, I like oxbow stirrups because it's

This is a cutting horse saddle, with a full-double rigging, that I often use to saddle colts for the first time because it's light and I can lift it onto a colt with one hand. I won't necessarily use it for the first ride, especially if it does not fit a colt.

easier to keep my feet in them. However, 2½-inch bell stirrups are more comfortable for riding all day, such as when you are gathering cattle. A lot of people use regular stirrups for breaking colts, and they do have one advantage: If you lose them, they are easy to find. Oxbows are easier to keep but difficult to pick up if you do happen to blow them.

17

Of these three cinch rings, the order of my preference is right, left, and center. The round-shaped ring with a round surface (center) has a very small surface next to the horse. Consequently it puts all the pressure in a very small area and is more likely to sore a horse. Many round cinch rings also have a little edge that can cut.

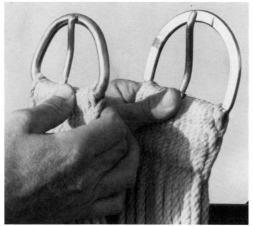

Here's a close-up of two cinch rings shown in the larger photo. I like the flat-sided ring (right) best because it's not as apt to sore a horse. The ring on the left would be my second choice.

Cinches

The front cinch should be strong so it won't break. When the strands start breaking, replace the cinch. That's better than replacing yourself. Broken strands can also make the cinch narrower, and then it will be more likely to sore the horse. I like to use a cinch that's at least 5 inches wide, because a wider width is less likely to sore a horse.

I like the material of the cinch to be soft, like mohair. You can go to a tack store and see some cinches that are made of a rough material, and you want to avoid those. If they are rough to your touch, they are

rough to a horse. Fleece cinch covers are not bad, but you must keep them clean. Because fleece cinches have a tendency to slip, I believe you have to cinch your horse a little tighter, also.

Keep in mind that a colt might still get some cinch sores even if the cinch is wide enough. That's because his skin is tender and not used to the pressure. If your colt does get some sores, put salve on them to keep them soft and help them heal. If you have to keep riding him, slip some sheepskin between the cinch and the sores, or use a sheepskin cinch cover. A piece of inner tube over the cinch also works well.

If you only have one saddle, but ride several horses, you might need several cinches of varying lengths. I think it's better to have a cinch that's too long, rather than one that's too short and puts the cinch rings way down low. Both cinch rings should always be above the elbows of the horse to help secure the saddle properly and to prevent sores from the rings. If the cinch is a little too long, it just means the rings are closer to the saddle, and the cinch is covering a wider area, which is good.

The design of the cinch rings is also important. A flat-sided ring will not sore the horse as much as a round or oval ring.

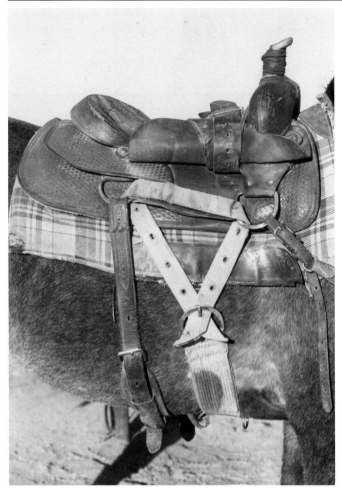
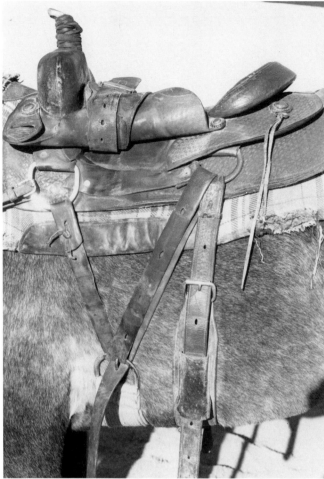

Maybe it's because the flat ring has a larger surface area, whereas a round ring always has a little edge to it somewhere. Some cinch rings also taper down, and they cut into a horse.

Many cinch rings have tongues in them, and I prefer that the tongue connect to the bottom of the ring. Some tongues are attached to a bar across the middle of the ring. I don't like that because it's harder to thread the latigo through, and that bar has probably been welded in or cast, and is just something else that can break.

Here in Arizona, the heat indirectly causes a lot of cinch sores. A horse gets hot and sweaty, and if the cinch is dirty, it can gall him quickly, especially if he has tender skin. So I wash my cinches frequently. I'll wash them in a bucket, using a detergent, and I rinse them *thoroughly*. Then in the last rinse, I'll add some fabric softener to make the cinch soft and loose. Otherwise it will be stiff after it dries and might irritate the horse until it loosens up.

Most young horses don't have good withers yet, and the saddle has a tendency to ride forward, like it does on a mule.

This pulls the cinch forward, which can irritate some of the tender skin just inside the elbows. This is another reason for keeping the cinch clean.

I always use a back cinch because it stabilizes the saddle. If a colt bucks, the back cinch holds the back of the saddle down, minimizing movement so it's not as likely to kick you out of the saddle. Even if I know a colt is not going to buck, I still use a back cinch so he gets used to it right away. I want a colt to understand what a back cinch is so that later on, if his owner uses a double-rigged saddle on him, he's not going to get in a storm and maybe hurt his owner.

I do have a pet peeve about people who ride with a back cinch, but don't snug it up against the belly. Instead, they leave about 4 to 6 inches of slack. In the first place, the back cinch doesn't do any good if it's loose. Secondly, it's dangerous because it can catch on something, like a branch from a bush. The horse can get a hind foot caught in it if he kicks at a fly, or kicks forward if he happens to buck.

All kinds of bad things can happen with

If you have a colt, or horse, that gets a cinch sore right behind the elbow, these photos show how you can rig your cinch to move it back. You can keep on riding him while the sored area heals. If you have a saddle that puts the cinch too close to the elbows, you could rig it this way to move the cinch back. I'll also ride some colts with a britchen—if they have no withers, a big belly, and I can't keep the saddle in place.

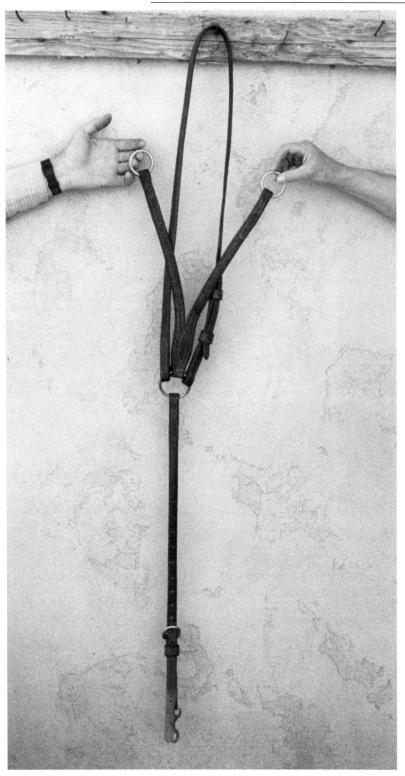

This is the type of running martingale I use.

a back cinch, so if you are going to use one, cinch it up snug against the belly so it can do its job and is safe. Otherwise, you might as well take it off.

Breast Collars

I use a breast collar for several reasons: 1/ so a colt finds out what it is and gets accustomed to it; 2/ to help keep the saddle in position, especially on young horses that don't have the best withers in the world; and 3/ so I don't have to tighten my cinch as much. Since the breast collar helps keep the saddle in place, I don't have to cinch the horse in two to keep my saddle where I want it.

Running Martingales

Even though I ride with a breast collar, I use a separate running martingale—instead of a fork attached to the breast collar or cinch. One that is only forked from the cinch isn't safe because when you have a lot of slack in your reins, or your horse stumbles, or puts his head down to drink, there's so much slack in the fork he can step over it. The running martingale I use attaches to the cinch and has a neck strap to prevent this.

The problem with using the fork from the breast collar is that it restricts the distance I can move each rein, both up and down and from side to side. A regular martingale gives me more freedom of movement.

Though I like a martingale, I don't ride with one all the time, because it has a tendency to let you get a little lazy. In other words, you can rely too much on the martingale helping you put a correct headset on a horse, instead of doing it with your hands and legs.

When properly adjusted, the rings on a running martingale should reach high enough so they are not putting constant pressure on the mouth.

Riding with a martingale all the time has a tendency to let you get a little lazy.

3 CATCHING A HORSE

Horses start sizing us up the moment we approach them.

WHAT: Getting a halter and lead rope on the horse.

WHY: Can't ride him without catching him first.

HOW: Several methods, depending on age of horse and how much he has been handled. Foal, use dam to corner him. Green horse, use panels to make squeeze chute. Gentle but smart horse, use grain, small pen, or whip-break him.

PROBLEMS: Horse might try to run over or kick you. He might come up for grain, then bolt away. He might not let you anywhere near him.

MOST TRAINING books start with a horse that you can catch, lead, and maybe tie up. But some people are starting from scratch and have problems getting their horses to the point where those other

This mare, who is easy to catch, has a month-old foal that's never been handled since foaling. They are kept in pasture, so we used several pipe panels to form a catch pen to make it easier to catch the foal.

books start. If you have a horse that you can catch, lead, and tie up, you can probably skip these next three chapters. But I encourage you to read them because each step in this book ties into the next. Just as in building a pyramid, the overall structure will be weak and fragile if you leave out key building blocks. When I get problem horses in for training, I determine which of the building blocks or basics has been left out, or maybe is just rusty. I then fix or teach the basics to the horse. Whether the horse is young or old, it's a good bet that any problem relates to one of the simple basics. If you teach the basics to your colt now, you will have a solid foundation to fall back on if you have a problem in the future.

All horses react to what we do. Two people could walk into a pen to catch a horse and the horse would react in two different ways. Some people can catch horses easier than other people can. If you sent a big, aggressive man in to catch a timid, scared horse, he'd fail. But give a 10-year-old girl the same opportunity and she would probably succeed.

Horses start sizing us up the moment we approach them. To stay on top of things, we should start analyzing them at the same time to measure their reactions to us. Any work you do with a horse makes an impression on him and sets the standard for what he expects from you. This impression will have an effect on his willingness to be worked with and ridden later on.

Whether you are trying to catch a foal that's never been caught, or an older horse that doesn't care to be, they both will learn from how you do it. The trust and respect which you instill in them now will have a direct influence on whatever you do with them next.

Here are several examples of how to catch horses of different ages and at different stages of training.

Foal

The sooner you start working with a foal, the easier it will be. For example, many foals receive imprint training immediately after they are foaled.

To catch a suckling foal, it's best to put the mare and foal in a stall or small pen. Use the mare to maneuver the foal into a corner or against a fence. If you have a

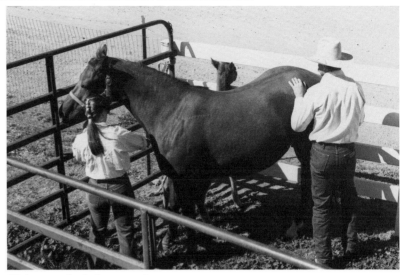

We've got the foal cornered.

My sister, Penny Debrito, moves the mare so I can catch the foal.

This is a typical reaction with foals being caught the first time or two. Although I've got hold of the tail, I'm careful not to pull on it or do anything else that might injure it.

While I hold the little guy, Penny slips the halter on.

This mare is not too concerned about her foal being handled, but with some exceptionally protective mares you have to be very careful they don't hurt you. The next chapter covers teaching this foal to lead.

The fastest, easiest, and safest way I know to halter an older horse that's loose is to haze him into a small pen or working chute.

helper, have him stand behind the foal, blocking his rear exit. Then you approach him from the front and catch him by putting one arm under his neck, right at his chest, and grasp his tail right at the base with your other hand.

Your arm under his neck prevents him from lunging forward. If he tries to back up, lift the tail until he stops. But be careful; if you lift the tail too high or too hard, you can injure it, perhaps permanently.

When you are holding the foal, stand close to him. You need to keep a firm hold, but should relieve some of the pressure when he's standing quietly. If you keep lifting the tail after he's stopped backing up, you'll just make him go forward. Relax, and make a good first impression. Let him know there's no reason to be afraid while you slip the halter on him.

After a foal has been weaned, you can use the same method, substituting a gentle horse for the mare. But it will be more difficult as the foal will be a lot stouter. What I'll do is reach over the horse and slip a halter on the foal. You can sometimes use this same method with yearlings on the smaller side.

Yearlings and Older

The older and larger the horses are, the harder it is to confine them. Even if they were halter-broke as weanlings, they may not want to be caught, and they have the size to push over and through things, including you. You can always spend a couple of weeks easing up to one of these horses and feeding him grain, but people usually need the horse caught quicker than that.

The fastest, easiest, and safest way I know to halter an older horse that's loose is to haze him into a small pen or working chute, like the ones you'll find at rodeo grounds. Not many people have bucking chutes available, but you can improvise with portable panels. How to set up the panels will vary according to the situation.

If the horse is in a pasture or large pen, I would form a small pen with the panels. I would put his feed and water in there— until I could eventually close the gate and trap him in the pen. If I still couldn't catch him, I would begin removing panels to make the pen smaller and smaller, squeezing the remaining panels together until I had the horse confined.

A diagram showing how to build a small pen in one corner of an arena or pasture to trap an uncatchable horse.

This sequence of photos shows how you can run a horse into the catch pen. George and I hazed this Paint down one side of a big arena, and he's heading right into the pen. George is sprinting to swing the pipe panel over and shut the colt in.

If the horse is already in a small pen, I would use panels to build a wing away from the existing fence (if it's a solid fence; don't do this with wire, especially barbed wire). I would swing the panels of the wing around the horse and back to the fence. Then, it's easy to slide the panels together until the horse is confined. (If the horse is in a wire pen, you can put panels inside the wire, to protect the horse from the wire.)

Some helpful hints: Have plenty of help. If you can, move slowly and quietly when easing the horse into the wing. If you move him in too fast, he could bounce back out before you can close the panels. And always make sure the panels are fastened securely to the existing solid fence.

This method of catching is safest for the horse because he's confined and won't get himself hurt while running, such as slamming through a fence. It's also the safest for you because there is a panel between you and the horse. However, don't take advantage of the situation, or let your guard down and relax. Take your time and show some respect for the horse. If you don't get in a fight with him on this first lesson, he won't be looking for a fight later.

It's never advisable to leave a halter on a

George swings the panel shut.

Sometimes when a horse finds himself trapped like this, he surrenders and you can easily catch him. If he doesn't, you can remove a panel and make a squeeze chute, as George is doing here.

The colt eyeballs freedom, but he can't do much . . .

. . . and it's easy for me to halter him.

loose horse because of the danger of it catching on something. Many horses have been killed or seriously injured as a result of their halters getting hung up on something. However, if you are going to start working to gentle this horse you've just caught, you might want to leave the halter on for a few days.

Make sure it fits snugly, but not too tight. You don't want it so loose he could rub it off because then you'd have to start all over again. If it's too loose, it's also more apt to hang up on something. He could even catch a back foot in it while scratching an ear. Yet you don't want it so tight it cuts into him. Also make sure that the stall or pen in which you leave him has nothing protruding that can snag the halter.

With a horse this green, you should also snap a long lead rope to the halter and let it drag. Otherwise, with just a halter on the horse, you still won't be able to walk up and catch him. The length of the rope should be in relation to the size of the pen. The bigger the pen, the longer the rope.

The rule of thumb: The rope should be long enough that you can walk into the pen and pick it up without chasing after it or your horse. I suggest using a ¾-inch cotton or nylon rope because it's easier to hang on to than a smaller rope. Because this rope is so much longer than a normal lead rope, be very careful not to get tangled in it. Also make sure there is nothing in the stall or pen that the rope can get caught on and trap the horse.

Hard-To-Catch Young Horse

Young horses that have been caught a number of times, but still haven't gentled down yet, can wise up to your training and be even harder to catch. Horses learn by repetition. You repeat their lessons until they form a habit. No matter how

26

With a horse not accustomed to being haltered, once you get him caught, practice slipping another halter on and off several times.

This gets him used to your right arm going over his neck, and the halter sliding up his nose.

time-consuming it may be to teach a green horse desired behavior, it's always easier to deal with it now rather than later.

If your horse remains hard to catch, you'll be starting off every training session on the wrong foot. You'll intimidate him if you bully him around, or you will create a monster if you are too passive. Somewhere in between you gain mutual respect.

Sometimes the answer to catching him is as easy as putting him with other horses that are easy to catch. If the easy-catchers stand quietly while you walk up to them, it won't be long before the hard-catcher will do the same.

Then there is always the famous grain-bucket trick. One rattle of this bucket can change the direction of a stampede and the horses' attitude of "let's get out of here" to "me first, me first."

Graining works especially well on timid or scared horses. They will begin to associate being caught with getting grain,

which they like. But this ploy doesn't always work with a smart horse because he might grab a mouthful and then run off. In this case, when you do catch him, let him finish the grain, maybe brush him, then turn him loose. Do this periodically. Then he won't always relate catching to working, and he will be more receptive to being caught. After the horse is easy to catch, I would stop using grain.

No matter how hard the horse is to catch, never lose your temper and jerk on him after he's caught—even if you are mad enough to sell him to Alpo. If he's afraid of being caught, getting after him when you finally catch him only confirms his fear and will make him even harder to catch next time.

If you have a green horse that will almost let you catch him before he moves away, confine him to a safe pen and let him drag a lead rope. (It's too dangerous to do this if he's in pasture.) He soon learns that you can easily catch him anytime you

With an exceptionally hard-to-catch horse, you can leave him in a safe, small pen, haltered and dragging a long lead rope that you can easily reach. This is a BLM mustang mare. I let her drag a lead rope several days until I could easily catch her. Always remember, however, that it's dangerous to leave a halter on a loose horse and should only be done in a safe area and only when absolutely necessary.

walk into the pen. He'll find that running off or sticking his head in the corner does no good. In a short time he will accept being caught, and a good habit has been formed.

Here's a helpful hint for getting this type of horse accustomed to being haltered. When you go to catch him, carry an extra halter and slip it on over the one he's already wearing. This gets him used to your right arm going around his neck and the halter sliding up his nose. If it startles him and he tries to leave, you can hold him with the lead rope. Repeat this every time you catch him for several days. Horses learn by repetition. Soon the horse will stand quietly for haltering, and you no longer will have to leave one on him.

Older Hard-To-Catch Horses

Sometimes I have hard-to-catch horses brought to me that were started by someone else. They either never learned properly at the beginning, or they don't like the way they are worked after being caught. Usually giving a new horse a couple of days to work into my program is all that's needed. But if he's gotten away with it for quite a while, sometimes I have to persuade him there's an easier way. One method I use is whip-breaking.

This sounds like an extremely harsh method, but it's not. And about the only time you use this method is on the horse

28

that sticks his head in the corner of a stall or pen. You are rightfully afraid to go around his rear end to reach his head because he might kick. Or, he may let you get up to his withers, and then turn and run off.

A horse cannot kick you if he's facing you, and this is where whip-breaking works so well. Actually, you can use a broom, rope, or whip; it just needs to be long enough so you can tap him on the butt and stay out of kicking range. With the horse in a small pen or stall, and your back to the gate or door, you can step out in a hurry if things go awry.

When I think I'll need to use this method, I'll take a whip with me, but will first try to catch the horse. If he turns his tail toward me, I'll cluck to him and ask him to move. With his head facing away from me, whichever way he moves will be toward me. So if he takes a step toward me, I'll quit clucking. The next time I cluck, if he turns toward me again, I'll back up a step; that is his reward. But if he doesn't respond to the cluck, or if he turns away from me, I'll tap him lightly on his hindquarters. I never tap him on the legs because that would encourage him to kick.

I'll tap him as many times as it takes to make him move toward me. As soon as he takes just one step, I'll quit tapping. Even if he just turns his head and looks at me, or gives any indication that he might be thinking about turning toward me, I'll quit tapping.

I'll wait a moment, and then ask him again by clucking, then tapping. By clucking first, I give the horse a chance to turn without tapping him. He then learns that after I cluck, I tap him; to make the tapping stop, he turns toward me. Pretty soon he'll turn toward me as soon as I cluck. He's anticipating the tap and beating me to the punch. This is good.

I'll give a horse an extra chance to turn around before I'll tap him. I want him to learn that if he turns around he won't get tapped. This way, I don't have to carry a whip with me every time I go to catch him.

Don't hit him any harder than you have to. If you come on too strong, you could drive him over or through the fence, or panic him if he's in a stall. Go slowly and quietly, and look for any sign of his moving towards you. If you stop tapping at the slightest movement, he'll learn to make that move to get relief. Soon the horse will make a bigger move, more quickly, to maintain the relief. When he does turn toward you, pet him and let him know that not only was it the right thing to do, it was a good thing to do.

Roping

I only mention roping here because it is one way to catch a horse. But if you don't know how to rope horses, don't try it. After your first throw and miss, the horse knows what's going on and he's not going to just stand there for your next throw. You'll probably run him over the fence before you get him roped. Or if you are lucky enough to catch him, he might stampede if he's never been roped before.

Roping can be the fastest and easiest way to catch a horse. But if you don't know how, it can make things a lot worse. If you have a friend, or a friend of a friend, who thinks he can, don't let him. It's just free practice for someone who won't have to pay for the outcome.

Don't get me wrong—I'm not against roping. When the situation calls for it, I don't hesitate to get my rope. But with all the ways I have explained to catch a horse, I doubt if you'll ever need to rope a horse.

A horse cannot kick you if he's facing you, and this is where whip-breaking works so well.

29

4 LEADING

A horse that follows goes only where you go. A horse that leads goes in the direction the halter is being pulled.

This illustrates a colt leading well . . . he's not lagging back, or getting ahead of me.

WHY: It's convenient; teaches manners; horse learns to stop, back up, stand still; learns respect for the halter; is a prerequisite for learning to longe.

HOW: Learning to follow and give to pressure; butt rope; girth rope; ponying.

PROBLEMS: Lazy horse or nervous horse; spooky horse; runs by you or drags back; leans on you.

THERE ARE lots of horses that have been broke for years that have never learned to lead. Instead, they have only been taught to follow, which is fine if they will follow you everywhere. But most of these horses stop following when they are being asked to go where they don't want to go.

A horse that follows goes only where you go. A horse that leads goes in the direction the halter is being pulled. A good example is the horse being loaded in a trailer. He's standing just outside the trailer, with the lead rope over his neck and you beside him. You can cluck to him and pull the lead rope forward, but he won't get in. But as soon as you walk into the trailer in

1/ *This is the colt we caught in the previous chapter (his dam is still in the pen, behind me). Initially, I want him to take just one step forward in response to light pressure on the lead rope. Here, there's slack in the rope.*

2/ *I apply very light pressure, and as soon as he takes just one step . . .*

front of him, he loads right up.

Learning to lead is usually the first training most horses get, usually when they are weanlings. Because you want your horse to accept being trained, it's important that you teach him how to *learn.* Horses are always easier to train if they are relaxed and trying to figure out what's wanted of them. They learn that you're going to help them. This is much better than jerking on a horse until he accidentally does what is required.

It's like taking a math test with multiple-choice answers. First question: 2+2= (how much). The answers: A/5; B/3; C/4; D/1. You haven't been taught how to figure this out, so you guess. The answer of 5 is wrong and you get slapped; 3 is wrong and you get slapped again; 4 is right and you don't get slapped. You didn't figure out the answer; you just kept guessing until the slapping stopped. You didn't learn anything.

But if you had learned how to count and add, this would have given you the background to figure out the answer, even if you had never been asked the question before.

The things we teach our horse in leading him are things that will set him up and

3/ *. . . I give him instant slack. Next, I move to his other side and ask him to take a step to his left in response to light pressure. I move from one side to the other, asking for a step in each direction until he takes it readily.*

4/ *Once the colt learns how to give to the pressure of the lead rope, then I'll use a butt rope or come-along. Here, there is slack in both ropes.*

5/ *I've asked the colt to step forward by first putting pressure on the lead rope. When I got no response, I put pressure on the butt rope.*

halter, he should not fight being tied up as badly as he would if he'd never been taught to lead.

I mentioned that there are horses that follow, but will not lead. However, learning to follow is a good start toward learning to lead, and there are a couple of ways you can do this. For example, a suckling foal can get a good idea of how to lead by following his mama. Slip a halter on him, as explained in the previous chapter; then you can either lead the mare and the foal, or ride the mare and pony (lead) the foal.

The foal might get a little upset when he feels pressure from the halter, but when he sees mama leaving, he'll come right along, because the mare means security. Pretty soon, he'll catch on to what a tug of the lead rope means.

You can also do this with a weaned colt as long as you use a gentle horse that will not bite or kick the colt, or get upset when the colt pulls back. Since you will not be able to hold the colt with your hand, you'll have to dally the lead rope around the saddle horn. If you are not experienced at doing this, and if your horse isn't used to the pull of a rope on the saddle horn, don't try it. Work with the colt on the ground.

If you are successful in ponying the colt, remember that he has only learned how to follow; you still need to teach him how to lead.

Teaching a colt or young horse to lead is not simply a matter of pulling on the lead rope to make him move forward. His instinctive reaction will be to brace against the pull, and perhaps to even run backwards. With this method, you are not teaching him anything constructive; you are simply matching your strength against his to make him move forward. As he grows up, he will have the advantage of size and strength.

Try this instead. Stand 6 to 8 feet in front of the colt, and a little to one side, not directly in front of him. It's harder for the horse to brace if you pull him a little to the side. (Once he gets the idea, you can pull from any angle.)

Although I use the term *pull,* you don't actually want to pull. Instead, just put enough pressure on the rope to take the slack out and make the colt a little uncomfortable. If you pull real hard and make the colt really uncomfortable, he'll fight

help him learn to longe and drive, the same as driving will prepare him for riding. The manners learned at this stage are very important. Not only does the horse learn to lead, but he finds out he can't drag you, or run by you. He learns what whoa means. He learns respect for the halter—to give to the pull, not to fight back.

Last but not least is the back-up. All too often this is forgotten or neglected. But it can be taught when the horse learns to give to the halter. Backing up plays an important role in the control of your horse, and being in control is what this book's all about.

Teaching a horse to lead will help later on when you begin tying him up. Because he has learned to give to the pull of the you more.

The less pressure the colt has on him, the better he thinks and the quicker he'll move in the direction you want. To keep from using too much muscle, I sometimes hold the rope with only my thumb and one or two fingers.

Once I have pressure on the rope, I consider my hand a barrier (to the colt moving any farther away from me). He will fidget around, and finally take a step toward me—either on purpose or by accident. No matter which, I give him instant slack—his reward.

If I was literally pulling on him when he took a step toward me, my reflexes wouldn't be fast enough to give him instant relief—and he wouldn't have learned anything. All animals learn faster when the reward is instantaneous.

I keep repeating this until the colt readily takes a step toward me as soon as he feels light pressure from the lead rope. I do not ask him to step straight ahead until he will readily take a few steps to each side in response to just a light pull. If at any point he stalls out and I have trouble, I go back to leading him from side to side.

If the colt is quiet or lazy, I'll only work him for a short time. I'll quit asking him before he quits trying. If the colt is really wild or scared, I'll work him in a small pen (15 by 15 feet) to ensure control of the situation. A colt is not as apt to run if he has no place in which to run and if you don't put pressure on him.

If the colt moves backward, I will have to follow him around, but my pressure on the lead rope remains the same. Sooner or later he'll stop backing up. I keep the same amount of pressure on the lead rope until he takes a step toward me. Whether he does it deliberately or accidentally, I instantly give him slack. Even if it was accidental, he will quickly figure that he gets relief from the pressure when he takes a step toward me.

You might be able to lead some colts around your corral in only a day, while others might take a little more time. If it takes an extra week, that's okay. One week now won't mean anything when this colt is 7 years old. I'd rather take the time now to do it right than fight him the rest of his life. I'll give him all the time in the world to learn something. But if you get a colt that's not interested or is just lazy, you might need a little help.

6/ As soon as he takes a step forward, I give him slack instantly.

7/ Again, I've asked the colt to step forward . . .

8/ . . . and again, I reward him with slack. Having the mare behind me encourages him to step forward.

9/ But he's also got to learn to move away from the mare when I ask him to. I'm applying light pressure.

10/ He doesn't take much of a step, but it's enough and I reward him with slack. If you follow this procedure and work with a foal a little bit every day, he'll be leading well in just a few days.

Butt rope or come-along. This is a rope that goes around the colt's rump, which you can pull to encourage him to take a step. Some people like to use it immediately when teaching a colt to lead, but I prefer to teach him how to give to the pressure of the lead rope first. Then he's learning to think things out.

I like a loop that fits around the colt's rump, and which is fixed so it can't close tighter when I pull on it. I also like the end of the rope to run back through the halter so if the colt runs by me, it doesn't slip off, and so it always pulls in the direction of the halter.

When I begin using a butt rope, I always ask the colt to step forward by first putting light pressure on the lead rope. If he doesn't respond, I'll tug on the butt rope, and that gets him to move. As soon as he does, I put slack in both ropes as his

reward. Pretty quick, as soon as I pull the lead rope, he'll start walking because he knows the butt rope's coming. Usually after just a few sessions with the butt rope, he'll know what I want and I can stop using it.

Girth rope. This is a rope that goes around the colt's body, just behind his withers. I make a loop that draws down when it's pulled on, and slackens when released. The honda lies under the colt's belly and the rope is brought up between the front legs and through the halter. This gives you better direction when you pull it.

The principle of using this is the same as with the butt rope. Ask first with the lead rope, then tug on the girth rope, and release when he steps forward. I don't use a girth rope often, but it works well and is another alternative if other methods fail.

Learning Manners, Whoa, Etc.

Now that the colt has an idea of what leading is, he needs not only to learn manners that make him a pleasure to lead, but also things that will help him to longe later on.

Whoa is the most important thing you will ever teach your horse. It helps keep you in control, and it's a lesson you will work on throughout his training. And you'll be glad how well he has learned what whoa means when you get on him the first time.

Since a colt can only learn one thing at a time, I wait until he's leading well before I teach what whoa means. When he's just learning to lead, it will confuse him to be led five steps, then told whoa to stop. Just when he thought he was doing right, you change things and make him stop. Always give a colt or horse time to learn each cue or command before you go on to the next one.

The first few times you work with your colt and ask him to whoa, it should be done without distractions. Depending on how much control you have, you can work in a barn aisle, small pen, or alongside a fence.

If the colt is quiet or timid, he will usually stop when you say whoa. If not, a light tug on the lead rope should help. Whenever you want to stop, always say

In teaching a horse to lead properly, I'll ask him to step forward in response to pressure from the lead rope in my right hand. If he doesn't respond, I'll reinforce my request with a tap from the whip.

whoa. He will soon relate the verbal cue to the physical cue—the tug on the lead rope. After a while, you can just say whoa and he will stop.

To start him moving again, I cluck to him and start walking. Soon he associates the cluck with moving.

The only verbal commands I ever use are whoa and a cluck. The horse, however, is capable of learning more commands, like walk, trot, and lope, and you can certainly use them when you ask for transitions.

When you say whoa, it should be a soft, relaxing sound. That puts the colt in the right frame of mind to stop. A cluck can be a more abrupt or sharper sound encouraging him to move, or to move faster.

When I stop a colt that's just learning whoa, I let him stand for maybe 30 seconds before moving off again. Stopping, then starting again right away will confuse the colt, and the real meaning of whoa— to stand still—will not register. His reward for stopping is the chance to stand quietly. If he's nervous, you might rub his neck.

However, it's equally important that you not let him stand too long, as he might start to fidget. Build gradually to his standing quietly for a longer time.

Back-up. To most people, the back-up is not essential, especially when working with a foal or yearling. You can longe, drive, and ride your horse without it.

However, I put a high value on teaching a horse to back, even when he's still too young to ride. I want it on the horses I lead as well as ride. It's a useful maneuver for any-age horse to know—such as when backing out of a horse trailer.

As a general rule, if the horse backs well from the lead rope, he'll easily pick it up when you drive him, and it will be "old hat" when you finally ride him.

When you ask a horse to back up, he should back as easily as he leads forward. You shouldn't have to jerk on the halter, poke him in the chest, or nudge him on the ankles to make him back.

As in all phases of training, I ask for just a step or two back the first time. But I'll repeat the lesson four or five times during a 20-minute period. If the horse is doing well, I'll have him back five or six steps the first day. At this stage, there's no reason to back him any farther than this.

However, it's not just how far he will back that's important; how lightly and easily he does it are equally important. The only way for him to learn is through repetition, so make backing a part of your program whenever handling your horse.

To teach him to back, give a series of tugs on the lead rope. A steady pull can cause him to lean on it. Cluck as you tug to encourage him to move back. If necessary, you can push on his chest to encourage him to take the first step.

1/ In this sequence, I'm going to start teaching the colt to stop. He's leading well here.

2/ I say whoa, and I give the lead rope a light pull to ask him to stop.

3/ The colt continues to walk, so I say whoa and give another light pull.

4/ The colt takes one last step and stops. When a colt is first learning to stop, you might have to ask him two or three times before he catches on.

1/ A colt should learn to lead equally well from both sides. To make it easier for him, I've positioned him alongside a fence. I'm asking him to step forward in response to a light pull on the lead rope.

If he seems to have a problem, first make sure you are giving him ample time to respond, and you are not asking for too much too soon. Then if he's not improving, use a short whip or the end of the lead rope to tap him on the chest.

First, tug on the halter backward to give him the direction, then cluck to him; if he doesn't respond, tap him with the whip. As soon as he takes just one little step back, stop (his reward) and rub his neck or forehead. Then repeat the lesson. Pretty soon you'll tug and cluck, and he'll move before you have to tap. After a few days, he'll start backing as soon as you indicate "back" with the lead rope.

Note: Because I said to tap him, this is not written permission to rear back and clobber him. You only increase the stimulus a little at a time until you get a response. To ask him real easy with the lead rope, then real hard with the whip will only confuse and frighten the horse, possibly causing him to bolt and run away from you.

Turning both ways. This is something else that's usually neglected or forgotten. Because horses are normally led from the left side, it's always easier to turn that way when leading them. But a horse should turn to the right as well as he turns to the left, whether being led or ridden. He should also lead equally well with you on his left or right side. You never know when you might get in a jam some day and *have* to lead the horse from his right side. And it's amazing how many horses won't do this.

I have also ridden spoiled colts who have been walking over their owners for 2 years; they always circle the owners to the left, and have never been asked to turn to the right. Such a colt turns good to the left when I get on him, but must be suppled and taught how to turn to the right.

Make a point of turning your horse both ways when you lead him. You want him to give equally well to both sides of the bridle, so it stands to reason that he should give equally well to both sides of the halter.

Working on both sides of your colt or horse is also a practice that should continue throughout his training. It will save you valuable hours of training later on.

Walks Slow, or Drags

If a horse is hesitant or slow when you are leading him, it might be that he's a little intimidated by you and feels safer keeping his distance. Or, he could be lazy.

2/ He didn't respond, so I tapped him with the whip (but the camera didn't catch it) and he starts walking.

3/ Now he's moving right along.

1/ Leading lessons should also include learning to back up. Here, I've asked the colt to back in response to a light tug on the lead rope; I'm getting no response.

2/ He's trying to evade pressure from the lead rope by throwing his head up. I won't give him any relief from the pressure until he moves a foot backwards, which he is just starting to do.

3/ Now he's moving back more readily.

Whichever, if he understands the principles of leading, here's what I'll do.

I'll work in a barn aisleway or against a fence. With the horse parallel to the wall or fence, I will stand at his shoulder, on his left side. I move my arm (the one holding the lead rope) forward and cluck. He might be unsure of what I want, so I try it a few times, letting him think about it.

If he still doesn't move, I'll reach back with a whip (in my left hand) and tap him on the hip or hindquarters (not on the legs). With some horses, I only have to wave the whip behind them to get them to move. With the fence on one side, me on the other, and the whip encouraging him from behind, he moves forward.

If he jumps and goes by me, I don't discourage him or get after him. After all, he did what I asked. But the next time, I will try to control it. I will not tap him as hard, and will move with him. He will learn that a tap of the whip will follow the cluck, and therefore will begin to move at the sound of the cluck. It won't be much longer before he begins walking as soon as you do.

1/ This colt had been dragging back and so I tapped him with the whip. He's now too far ahead, but I don't want to discourage him from doing what I just asked.

2/ Instead, I pick up my pace to catch up with him. He had also slowed down a little and is in the right position now.

1/ In turning, the horse should not lean into you . . . he should maintain the correct distance from you.

Running By or Leading You

To me, a horse that pushes on the halter and walks ahead of me is more annoying than a slow leader. And a horse that's chargey and runs by me is even worse. Such a horse has no manners and is dangerous.

For a horse that walks just a little faster than he should, I will stop him and make him back up a few steps. I do this quietly, to just let him know that if he walks too fast, he will have to stop and back up.

With a horse that's a little more chargey, I will stop and back him repeatedly. I don't even wait until he gets ahead of me. As soon as he starts charging, I make him stop and back. I want to instill in his brain the fact that he should be thinking *back,* not *forward,* when I'm leading him. However, I just use a regular halter and lead rope to do this.

I do not use a lead chain except on those severe cases . . . horses that have no respect for the halter and try to run right through it. Then I run a chain over the nose, not under the jaw. If you are trying to stop a horse's forward motion, putting the chain over his nose makes more sense. I will also initially work this horse in a more confined area, such as a small pen, so I have more control. Again, I make this horse stop and back up when he just *thinks* about charging. But I use discretion, always giving the horse a chance to respond to a light pull before going to a heavier pull. As soon as I can, I switch back to a regular lead rope snapped into the halter ring.

Leaning Into You

There are times when insecure horses feel more comfortable and safe when next to you rather than 2 or 3 feet away. While you are leading them, they constantly lean into you, and sometimes try to walk right on top of you. This is not only bad manners, it's dangerous.

Because this type of horse is veering your way and pushing you to the left, some handlers will let him circle around them, and then head out again in the desired direction. Teaching a horse to circle to the right when being led helps to alleviate the problem; ask him to circle to the right when he starts leaning on you.

Lots of times I will use my arm and elbow to push him away from me when he gets too close. I don't like to use my hand because that might make him head-shy. Believe me, a horse knows the

Some handlers inadvertently cause their horses to walk too fast.

difference between a hand that pets him and an elbow that pokes him.

Some handlers inadvertently cause their horses to walk too close to them because they hold the lead rope right by the snap, and literally hang on to the halter. They feel this gives them more control. However, it encourages the horse to walk on top of you.

I like to lead my horses with at least 2 or 3 feet of slack. This puts a comfortable distance between us so we can walk without bumping into each other, yet still gives me plenty of control.

5   TYING UP

Learning to stand quietly is a very important part of a horse's education.

WHY: Teaches patience, respect for the halter; makes horse easier to work with; don't have to chase him around.

HOW: Use strong post and inner tube. Tie short and high, and so a horse can't untie.

PROBLEMS: Tying too short or too long, or to a bad post; won't lead up to post; unties himself; getting in front of him; getting finger caught in knot.

A LOT OF people ignore this part of their horses' training program because they are more concerned with getting on and riding. But learning to stand quietly is a very important part of a horse's education, regardless of how old he is.

Let's say there are a couple of 2-year-olds tied to a fence. One is standing quietly with slack in the rope; the other is pacing back and forth, pawing the ground,

This filly is properly tied. She's got on a stout halter and lead rope, and is tied with the right amount of slack and at the right height to a stout post.

and tugging on the lead rope. It's not a hard decision as to which one I'd rather ride: the one standing quietly.

This colt has already learned some of the things a broke horse should know, and he hasn't even had a saddle on him yet. Even though the post to which this colt is tied has a lower I.Q. than most trainers, it has been able to teach this colt a number of things in a relatively short amount of time.

This colt has learned that the post is not going anywhere, so neither is he. The second colt is still testing it. The colt I like has already learned patience, a quality that all horses must have in order to endure training. Patience is what the post teaches a horse. (Patience is also the main quality trainers should have when working with horses.)

In theory, if a horse has learned enough patience to stand quietly while tied, this patience will carry over to other activities. Simple things like standing still while we brush him, trim his feet, and get on and off him. Although tying him up will not teach him these things, it will give him the patience to learn them.

Tying up really helps when halter-breaking colts—after they have had their initial leading lessons. How? Sometimes our timing is not what it should be when teaching a colt to lead. For example, we might be pulling when we should be giving. The post has better timing than we do. When the colt pulls back, the post holds firm; when the colt moves ahead, the post gives him immediate relief from the pressure—his reward.

This amazing post can do this all day long to all of your colts, and doesn't need any help or even a lunch break.

After a colt learns to stand tied, he has respect for the halter and he's learned a good habit that transfers to when you are leading him: he will not pull away from you.

There are some owners who don't like to tie up their horses. They believe it's dangerous because the horse might smash them against the post or fence if he pulls back and then jumps forward. That's why you should not stand in front of a horse that might pull back. This relates to the No. 1 rule of working with horses: safety first. Never put yourself in a position where you might get hurt.

If a horse likes to pull back when he's tied, he may not have been tied long enough to get his Ph.D. (post-holding degree). If he does tie up well, but tries to pull back, it could be you are putting too much pressure on him; go a little slower in whatever you are doing.

This amazing post can do this all day long to all of your colts.

45

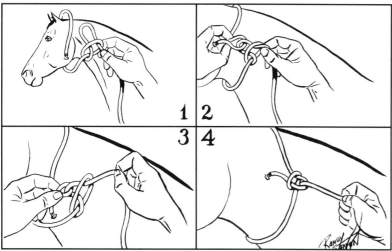

Here's how to tie a bowline knot: 1/ Pass the rope around the neck; then throw a simple loop in the standing part of the rope. 2/ Insert the free end of the rope through the loop formed; double back the end and hold this loop formed with thumb and forefinger of left hand. 3/ With the right hand, pull the standing part of the loop carefully, using an upward motion that will make the loop of the first knot slip over the loop in the left hand to form a perfect bowline.

This is how I'll normally tie a horse to a hitch rail. I take two wraps around the rail and tie with a slip knot; to finish the knot shown here, the tail of the rope should be tucked through the loop. With two wraps around the rail and the knot tugged down, the rope won't slide. And if the horse pulls back, the pressure is put on the wraps, not on the knot, which can still be jerked free.

Another reason why some people don't like to tie a horse: they feel that it will make the horse scared because he feels trapped. One reason we tie a horse is to get him used to it so he *won't* feel trapped and scared. The other reason is for our convenience. A horse that cannot be tied is a nuisance.

Learning to stand patiently is for the horse's safety and our convenience.

There are three basics to remember when tying a horse: 1/ Use a stout post, halter, and lead rope; 2/ Tie short and high; and 3/ Use a knot you can untie quickly, but which the horse cannot.

Stout post. Always tie a colt to something he cannot break or pull loose. It can be a tie ring securely anchored in a wall, or a fence post, or a single post. It should be strong enough to hold the horse if he fights being tied, so he won't injure himself if he rubs it or crashes into it. If it's a post in a fence, it should be a solid fence (never a wire fence) so he can't get any legs through it when he paws, kicks, or pulls back, and then lunges forward.

Some awful wrecks have happened when people have tied horses to movable objects. For example, I once saw a man tie his horse to an empty feed cart. The horse didn't like the cart and moved away from it. The cart moved with him. So the horse moved again—and the cart followed him. The horse took off running because he thought the cart was chasing him—which it did, twice around the barn before the cart disintegrated.

I admit you can tie an older horse to some things you wouldn't tie a green colt to. But since this book is about starting colts, we will proceed with that in mind.

If you tie to a fence, it's best to tie to a post, rather than a crosspiece, such as a board or plank. The latter can be pulled off if the horse sets back, and few things are more frightening than a scared horse running wildly still tied to a board.

The post should be strong enough so a horse can't break it, and it should be set deep enough in the ground so he can't pull it out. It should have no protruding nails or bolts, or sharp edges. Some people will stack tires on the post for added protection, but these really aren't necessary.

When teaching a horse to stand tied, use a stout halter and lead rope. If the horse pulls back and one or the other breaks, the horse could get hurt if he flips over back-

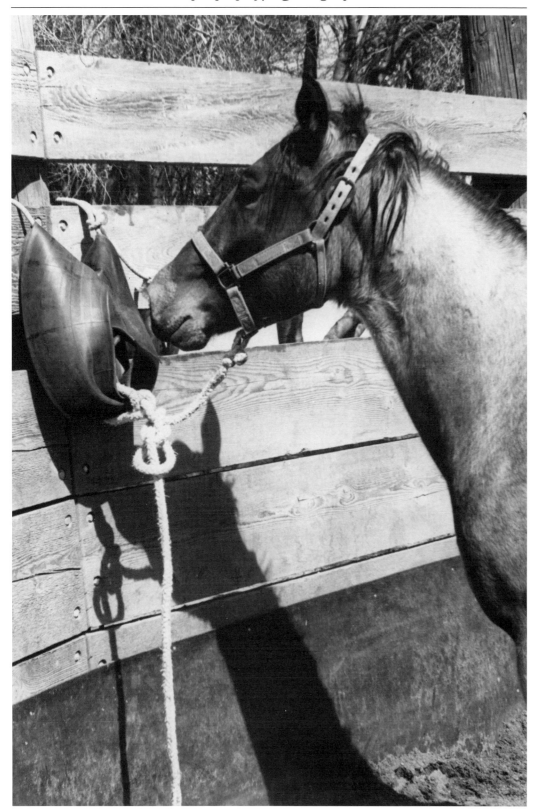

Here's how I'll tie a horse to an inner tube.

Always tie a colt to something he cannot break or pull loose.

47

Because the tube stretches, it gives relief to a horse testing the rope, but still holds him.

ward as a result of his momentum. Some horses have been killed as a result.

If the horse survives, he has learned that if he sets back, he can get free, and this is the beginning of a bad habit.

We have already talked about halters and lead ropes in the section on equipment, but briefly, a heavy-duty nylon halter with *good* hardware would be a wise choice. So would one of those rope-type synthetic halters with no hardware.

Depending on the size of your horse, a rope measuring ½ or ¾ inch in diameter should be strong enough. Cotton rope is soft and easier on your hands, but has a tendency to wear out faster because of its softness. Synthetic (nylon or poly) ropes hold up longer, and you can wear gloves to protect your hands.

Many times I will use an old nylon lariat rope to tie with because it has lots of stretch in it and takes a good-size truck to break it. When I do use a lead rope, I like one 7 to 8 feet long. I can find more use for a longer rope than a short one. A rule-

of-thumb: the wilder the horse, the longer the lead rope.

When I tie a colt or older horse that's never been tied before, I like to use an inner tube around the post and tie my lead rope into it. Because a tube stretches, it gives relief to a horse testing the rope, but still holds him. And we are trying to *teach* the horse, not hurt him. The extra stretch in the inner tube also minimizes chances of the halter or lead rope breaking.

When working with a horse that's never been tied before, don't just snub him up and stand there tying a knot. If he pulls back, you could get your fingers caught in the rope, or he could jump forward and hit you. And if your fingers are caught in the rope, chances are you'll be right there when he leaps forward.

What I do is run my rope through the inner tube or around the post, then tie it to the next post down the line. This puts me at a safe distance from the horse. I also take one or two dallies (wraps) around the post I'm tying to; then if the horse pulls back before I make my tie, the dallies will hold him.

Tying short and high. Now don't get carried away with these two words. Too much of anything is bad. I think a horse should be able to stand tied with his head in a comfortable position, and with slack in the rope. How much slack? About 1 to 2 feet is plenty. If you give him 3 feet of slack, he can actually move in a semi-circle with a 6-foot radius. If you are trying to do something with him, you'll find it irritating that he can move around so much.

A horse should never be tied with so much slack that he can get a front foot over the rope when he puts his head down. When he raises his head, the foot will go with it, and you've got a wreck in the making.

I like the rope to be tied at about the same level as the horse's withers, although some people tie at eye-level, which is okay. What you should NOT do is tie any lower than wither-level. Not only could the horse get a foot over the rope, but if he pulls back with any force, he can pull his neck down. This is a serious and sometimes permanent injury. If he's tied high, this usually won't happen.

The knot. Your knot should be one that you can untie quickly and easily, but the horse can't. To keep a knot from tightening down if the horse pulls back, I'll take two or more wraps around the post, then tie the knot. The dallies take most of the pressure.

You could also tie a bowline knot. You can't undo it in a hurry, but at least you can *always* undo it.

What about a slip knot? If a horse pulls back hard, a slip knot will tighten down so it won't slip—and therefore will be hard to untie. To eliminate this problem, I either take two wraps around what I'm tying to, or tie a simple half-hitch first and then tie the slip knot on top of it. Then if the horse pulls back, the pressure will be put on the wraps or the half-hitch, not on the slip knot—which can be easily jerked loose.

Sometimes I'll get a horse in that won't even lead up to the post. I will take a couple of wraps around the post, wait for him to take a step toward it, then take the

If a horse is so broncy I can't lead him up to the inner tube, I'll tie this ring into it, run the lead rope through the ring, and ease the horse up to it.

slack out. If necessary, I'll attach another long rope to my lead rope so I can get behind the horse and take the slack out as he moves away from me. I always do this slowly and give him time to think between moving and my asking him again.

If I have a horse that doesn't lead well, or is not safe to stand close to, I'll use a long rope, run it around a post, and gradually ease the horse up to it. Each time he takes a step forward in response to light pressure, I take up the slack.

Houdini horses. Some horses are very clever about untying themselves. You can tie several knots, one on top of another, but a Houdini horse will still get them undone, although it might take him five minutes instead of two. The secret to stopping this is to put the end of the lead rope where he can't reach it. What I do is take a couple of wraps around the post, then make my tie on the side of the halter. He can't reach it with his mouth, and if it's a good knot, he can't undo it by rubbing against the fence. Another way is to put the rope around the post, but tie the knot on down the fence at the next post.

Time. How long to leave a horse tied depends on the situation. The first time I tie a horse up, I might leave him there 10 to 30 minutes. I just want him to realize

When I have the horse where I want him, I tie off to the next post down the line. This is a BLM mustang mare.

what's going on—that he can't take the post anywhere. Then I'll increase the time over the next few days. I don't want to teach him this all at once.

It's like the first time we pick up his foot; we don't see how long we can hold it. We just pick it up and put it right back down. We increase the time as he learns so eventually we can hold it long enough for the shoer to trim it or tack on a shoe.

After about a week of tying him up, and if everything is going well, I stop using the inner tube. But if he's still testing whether he can pull the post out of the ground, I continue using it.

Regardless of whether he's tying well, I increase his tying-up time. I want to increase his patience so he is solid on tying up. If he's not doing well, I increase the time because he needs to learn that pawing and walking back and forth is not doing him any good, and that it's easier to stand quietly than to jump around.

Another factor: If the horse doesn't have the patience to stand tied for 15 minutes, he sure won't have the patience to listen to you try and train him for 30 minutes.

However, please ignore anyone telling you to leave your horse tied up all day and all night. First, it's not humane. Second, it's a lazy man's way of training to get a lot done in a short amount of time. You'll do more good by tying a horse up 4 hours a day for 6 days than by tying for 24 hours straight.

If you do tie a horse up all day, he should have a chance to eat in the morning, and you should offer him water several times during the day. Also use caution if it's extremely hot or cold. Tie him in the shade, or in a shelter of some type.

Also remember that colts should never be left unwatched while tied up. They are just like kids or puppies. A little black cloud called "mischief" hangs over their heads and rains on them as soon as you turn your back.

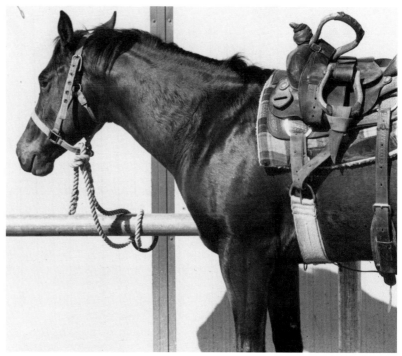

With a Houdini horse that unties himself, I tie the lead rope back into the halter. This photo also shows tying the stirrups up as an added safety precaution. Some horses, if they are tied too long, reach around to play with a stirrup, hook the lower jaw on it, and break the jaw. Note the horseshoe on this hitch rail so a tie rope won't slide. On the negative side, this rail is lower than I like, but it's okay for this mare since she is broke to stand tied.

Colts are just like kids or puppies. A little black cloud called "mischief" hangs over their heads.

51

6 LONGEING

For longeing I use a lightweight nylon longe line snapped to the halter ring.

WHAT: Working the horse at the end of a line in a circle around you.

WHY: Conditioning; getting the fresh off; bitting up; teaching voice commands; preparation for driving and riding; learning whoa; walking, trotting, and loping when asked.

HOW: Use whip; drive him from behind; give him only one way to go; step in front to stop; step back to bring him to you; emphasize whoa.

PROBLEMS: Horse faces you and won't move; will only go in one direction; won't stay out on end of line; walks up to you when he stops; won't stop.

LONGEING has several advantages that can benefit any horse, regardless of his age or stage of training. Some of the reasons for longeing:

1/ It takes the edge off a horse that hasn't been worked in a while or is feeling fresh.

2/ It can help teach manners and discipline, and response to the verbal command *whoa*.

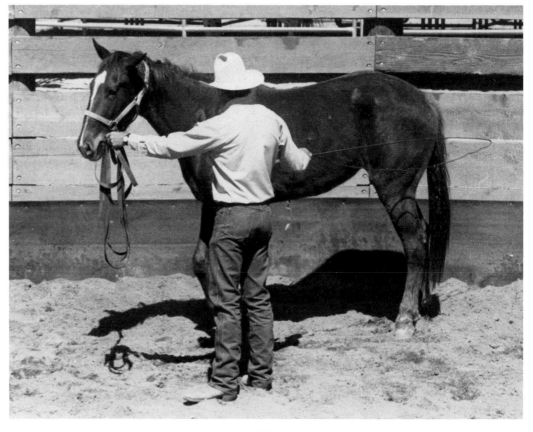

1/ This is a series of five photos showing how I start this mare longeing to the left. I hold the longe line in my left hand, the whip in my right, and stand alongside her.

2/ *I cluck to the mare and follow that up by tapping her on the rump with the whip to ask her to start walking. I also begin walking.*

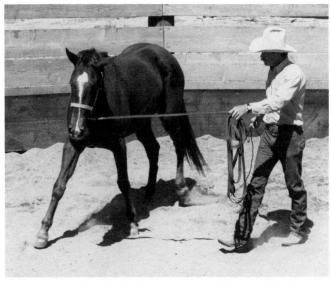

3/ *I encourage her, by clucking, to keep walking as I feed her more line. I try to stay opposite her rib cage or hip. If I get too close to her head, she'll probably stop.*

4/ *As I feed her more line, I position the whip so she can see it out of the corner of her eye. She's got her left ear cocked toward me, listening to me and "watching" the whip.*

5/ *The mare is moving out willingly at a nice trot . . . and I keep walking to maintain my position.*

3/ It can help develop a correct headset and light mouth on a horse that is bitted up.

4/ It can be used to condition and exercise a horse. (Note: Too much longeing, however, can create lameness problems in young horses.)

5/ It helps prepare a horse to learn how to drive.

Longeing can be done anywhere—in a pasture, large arena, or in a square or rectangular pen, but it's easiest to do in a round pen. A round pen gives you better control, and it has no corners into which a horse can duck and hide his head. It also provides a consistent circle in which the horse can travel.

If you just want the horse to exercise, you can turn him loose in the round pen and let him go. But if you want to teach him discipline and verbal commands, and get him ready for driving, you need to put him on a longe line. I use a nylon line and attach it to a regular halter. Specific longeing halters are made, in which the line attaches to a ring on the nosepiece, but I find that a regular halter works just fine.

I use a light line that's long enough so I can stand in the middle of the pen while the horse works around the perimeter. I also snap it to the ring underneath, not to the rings on the side. That way, when I ask the horse to change directions, I don't have to stop him and change where the line is snapped. Also, when I ask the horse to stop, I want a direct tug under his jaw, not on the side of his face.

When a horse has never been longed before, he will be confused when you step

1/ Here's a series in which I teach the mare to longe to her right. I hold the line in my right hand and the whip in my left. I have clucked to the mare and tapped her.

2/ She's moving, but looks a little confused. Just because she has learned to longe to the left doesn't necessarily mean it will be easier to teach her to move the other way. As with everything else in training a horse, you have to teach both sides. And if a horse is "left-handed," it can be especially difficult to teach him to longe to the right—and vice-versa.

to his side, cluck to him, and stand there while asking him to move. He's accustomed to your moving with him. So be patient, and proceed as shown in the photos.

If you are asking him to move to the left, hold the line in your left hand and the longe whip in your right. Switch when asking him to move to the right.

Stand by the horse's rib cage, cluck to

him, tap him on the rump with the whip, and ask him to move. As he begins moving, feed out the line; don't pull on his head, because that contradicts what you are asking him to do. Just give him slack and let him go, moving at whatever gait he chooses so he gets used to moving around you in a circle.

If the horse is confused and hesitant, keep asking; he will begin moving soon.

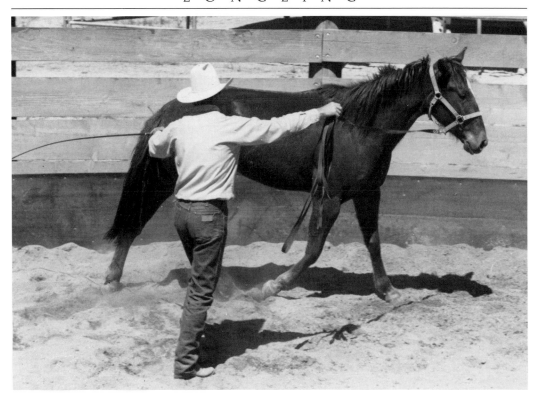

3/ Notice my position; this is about where you should be when teaching a horse to longe.

4/ Now she's doing better, and I'm starting to feed more line to her.

Your position in relation to the horse's body is very important. As he begins to move, you have to keep moving to stay opposite the horse's hip.

Your position there encourages him to move forward. If you are standing opposite his head, it's as if you are blocking his path, even though you are not directly in front of him, and as a result, he's likely to stop and face you.

When this does happen, move back to the hip position, and then ask him to move. Depending on the horse, you may have to be pretty fast on your feet, to stay opposite his hip, until he learns what he's supposed to do. Once he has, you should be able to stand in the center of the pen instead of walking around.

A word about the whip. You use it to *ask* the horse to go, not to abuse him. You

1/ I'm getting ready to ask the mare to stop, so I step toward her head.

2/ I say whoa, and tug on the lead rope.

3/ She takes a couple of more steps as she cocks her head toward me.

4/ For just learning how to stop, she did a nice job.

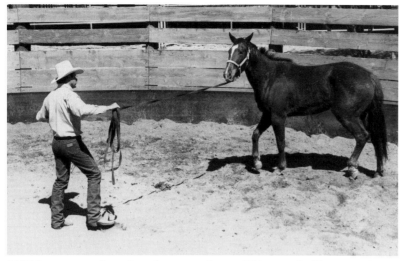

1/ *This sequence shows how I reverse a horse. This mare had been moving to the left, and now I want her to move to the right. First, I stop her, switch hands on the line and whip, then pull her toward me a few steps.*

2/ *As she steps toward me, I extend the line to my right, the whip to my left, and step to my left.*

3/ *I cluck to her, and tap her with the whip, if necessary.*

may have to hit him with it one time to let him know that it does sting and that it does mean go, but the next time, you may only have to pop it behind him so he hears the sound.

Also, always cluck to the horse before you tap him with the whip. Then the horse will learn that the whip follows the cluck, and pretty soon he'll start moving as soon as you cluck in order to avoid the whip. However, do not continually cluck, as the horse will begin to tune it out, and eventually will ignore it. Cluck just once or twice, then tap him with the whip if he doesn't start moving.

If he has already learned what whoa means from his leading lessons, you shouldn't have much trouble stopping him. Step toward his head, say whoa, and tug on the lead rope. If he doesn't stop right away, just keep saying whoa and tugging until you get him stopped.

Your goal is to stand in one position, say whoa, give a light tug (sometimes the whoa alone will stop the horse), and the horse will stop. If the horse is not paying attention to the tugging, you may have to increase the pressure. However, if that doesn't work and the horse is pumped full of energy, I will keep longeing him until he's tired and more willing to stop.

You'll notice that as the horse gets a little tired, he'll be eager to stop as soon as he hears you say whoa, or any other word that sounds like whoa. But if he's really excited and tearing around the pen, there's not much sense in asking him to stop because he's not going to listen to you, and you'll have to fight his head. So just let him keep going until he does get tired and wants to stop.

In fact, you could even use reverse psychology on him. If you have asked him to stop, but he ignores you, just stand quietly and let him keep going. Then when he shows signs of tiring and *wants* to stop, don't let him. Pop him with the whip and make him keep going a few more laps. Then when you finally say whoa, he'll want to stop and rest. As you repeat this exercise, he will become more responsive to the word whoa.

The first few times I ask a horse to stop, I don't worry how he stops as long as he comes to a halt. But as he learns to stop better, I'll begin asking him to stop and stay parallel to the fence, and not turn in and face me. It's a matter of manners and

4/ *She's about figured out what I want.*

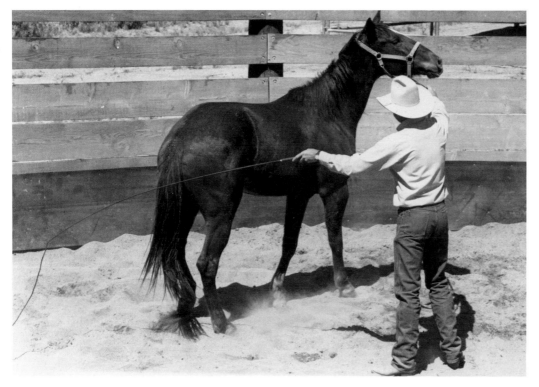

5/ *Now she's starting to move okay.*

1/ This series shows what I do if a horse turns and faces me after he stops. Here, I've asked the mare to stop.

2/ I gather up the line as I walk to her.

discipline for him to stop and stand in the same direction as he was traveling. After all, when I am driving and riding him later on and say whoa, I want him to stop and stand in his tracks, and not turn sideways. So I begin teaching that to him now.

When the horse does turn toward you, and most young horses will, walk up to him quietly, gathering up your line so you don't get tangled in it. Take hold of his halter and push his front end over so he is parallel to the fence, and tell him whoa. Then begin backing away from him, toward the center of the pen. If he takes a step toward you, repeat the lesson, until he will finally stand still while you move back to the center.

Always back away from the horse so you can watch him. If you turn around, he might follow you and you won't know it until you're back in the center of the pen. But if you're watching him, the minute he takes a step toward you, you can correct him.

Once you are back in the middle of the pen, do not let him stand there too long, as he won't have the patience to do it. Ask him to move on before he starts fidgeting and moves again. Build his patience by gradually asking him to stand there longer.

Pretty soon the horse will learn that when he stops, he's going to have to stay

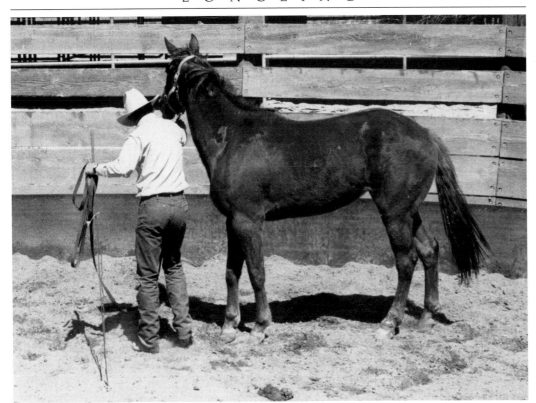

3/ I reposition her so she is parallel to the fence.

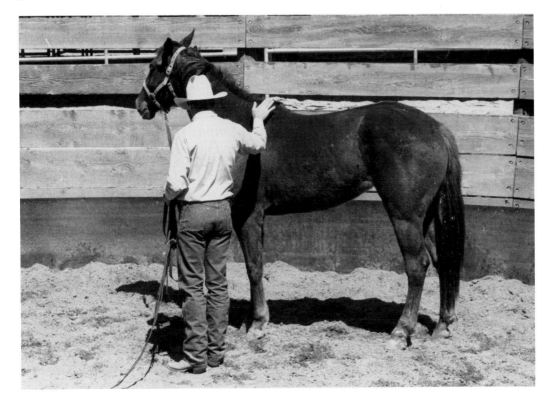

4/ I tell her whoa, then I back up to the center of the pen. If I were to turn around, she might follow me and I would not know it.

in the position you want. If he does turn toward you, he will learn that as you walk toward him, you're going to push him back into that position. In fact, some horses will move back into position as soon as you take a step toward them.

I don't believe a horse must longe perfectly to be a good riding horse. As long as he comes to a nice little stop and does not come walking in to me, I don't care if he takes a little step or two towards me. If he learns to stop and stand almost parallel to the fence, I'm happy. Making him stand perfectly straight is nit-picking, and I don't believe it's going to help him be a better riding horse.

The first several times I reverse the horse, I ask him to stop first. Suppose he's been moving to the left. After he has stopped and is standing, I pull him toward me a few steps, then move to my left, and extend the whip toward his right side. As he begins moving to the right, I step toward his right hip, and ask him to keep moving.

One problem in longeing is that some horses like to cut the corners. If this keeps up, pretty soon they are making small circles around you. To prevent this from happening, you can flip the longe line toward the horse's head to push him back out, or you can flick the whip toward him to make him move away from you and

hold the circle.

Another problem is the horse that likes to go only one way. With lots of longeing in his "bad" direction, he'll become more accustomed to traveling in that direction. But it can be a lot of work to get him moving that way because he'll probably keep turning and facing you.

When this happens, you should use the whip behind the horse, and ask him to move forward. Tap him with the whip if necessary. Once again, you keep moving in order to stay opposite his hip, and be sure to give him enough slack so you are not pulling on his head.

If a horse refuses to move away from you, then you haven't put enough pressure on him. At first, it might take a lot, but as he learns, he'll move away more readily.

If he succeeds in stopping and facing you, repeat the whole procedure, being careful not to lose your patience. If worst comes to worst, you might even have somebody lead the horse in his bad direction, while you handle the longe line, until the horse will willingly move that way by himself.

But usually if I stay far enough behind the horse, I can block his path if he tries to turn around. Then I am in a good position to move him in the direction I want him to go.

2/ This mare has gotten the message and is moving farther away from me.

3/ I give her more line as she moves out to the fence.

63

7 SACKING OUT

When I am sacking out a colt, there are two things I stress: control and safety.

WHAT: The process of introducing strange objects and activities to a horse in such a manner that he will accept them reasonably calmly.

WHY: To make the horse safer to work with.

HOW: By slowly and carefully introducing him to the feel of your hand, a brush, and a blanket.

PROBLEMS: Going too fast; showing him too much at one time; being too aggressive and scaring him.

THE TERM *sacking out* probably originated when cowboys long ago would take a gunny sack and rub it all over a colt to get him accustomed to the feel of being handled. In the old days, many colts ran loose on the range until they were four or five years old. Except when they were branded and/or gelded, they were never touched until the horse breaker ran them in and started working with them. Because they had never been handled, it was important that they get used to the feel of something being rubbed against them, and a gunny sack was handy to use.

Nowadays, most young horses are handled regularly as yearlings and 2-year-olds. Nonetheless, I feel that sacking out is still an important part of the training program. It makes a colt easier and safer to handle because he is gradually accustomed to things that might otherwise frighten him, such as the shoer trimming his feet, the vet giving him inoculations, and being saddled.

There is no way we can introduce a colt to every strange thing that might happen, such as a gust of wind blowing a paper bag at him. But the more situations we can put him in, the better he can handle anything that might happen.

Some people are critical of sacking out, no doubt because they have seen or heard of it being applied incorrectly. You can take a blanket or sack and rub it over a colt's back until he relaxes and enjoys it. Or you can thrash him with it until just the sight of it scares him. With the first method, you make things better; with the second, you make them worse. It's all in the application.

How much time to spend sacking out a colt depends on the individual colt—how much he has already been handled, and his age. If he's just a weanling, about all you do is accustom him to being handled so the horseshoer and veterinarian can work with him safely. He should stand quietly for his feet to be trimmed, and for inoculations and worming.

If he's a 2- or 3-year-old who is pretty quiet and gentle, has been handled a lot and maybe blanketed, it won't take long. I can sack out some colts, saddle them, and ride them on the first day. On the other hand, I've broke a number of BLM wild horses for customers, and it can take anywhere from 2 weeks to months to get them to the same state as barn-raised colts.

But they all come around sooner or later. It depends on three things: 1/ their mental makeup (temperament, intelligence, etc.); 2/ their previous handling, if any; and 3/ how I approach and apply their training now. Since I have no control over the first two, it's important that I take the time and do the last one right.

When I'm sacking out a colt, there are

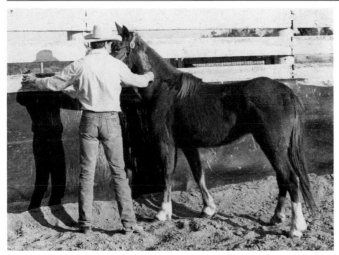

1/ This is a BLM wild mare that had been sent to me for gentling and breaking. I had been working with her for several days, and she was somewhat accustomed to my rubbing her with my hands when this sequence was taken of my picking up each foot for the first time. Approaching her at the shoulder is the safest place to be.

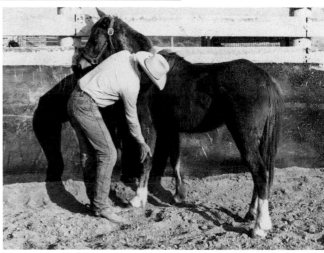

2/ After rubbing her a little bit on her neck and shoulder, I move my hand up and down her leg. I keep my left hand on her shoulder to serve as my early warning system so I can instantly feel if she starts to get nervous.

3/ She is standing quietly, so I reach for the fetlock and ask her to pick her foot up.

4/ She raises it a couple of inches.

5/ I hold it briefly.

6/ I put it right back down. That's all I want to accomplish at this stage.

7/ I move to her hip and rub her a little bit.

8/ I ask her to lift her back leg.

9/ She gives it to me willingly.

10/ Moving to her other side, I approach her carefully.

two things I stress: control and safety. I don't want to get hurt, and I don't want the colt to get hurt. If I have control, that means things should stay safe.

Depending on the colt and the situation, I may either tie him up or hold him while I sack him out. For someone who lacks experience, however, it would be best if the colt were tied. Otherwise, he can learn a bad habit by continually being able to move away from the handler, or even running off.

Even if a colt knows how to lead well and stand quietly when tied, this doesn't give me a license to force anything on him. I believe that the easier you can be with a colt, the quieter he's going to be. If you want him gentle after he's broke, you've got to break him that way. Any time you can teach him to do something in a nice, soft way, that's the way he will learn to do it. And remember it.

When sacking out, I take my time, ap-

proach him quietly, and watch for any indication that he's getting nervous or scared. When he does, I'll back off whatever I'm doing, and gradually work to regain his confidence, and assure him that there's nothing to be scared of.

I always start by using my hands. If I'm working with a colt that's never been handled much, a sack, saddle blanket, or even the feel of a brush might spook him. I approach him at the shoulder. Although you can get hurt standing anywhere around a horse, the shoulder is safer than any other place. If I'm farther forward, he could strike at me with a front foot or run over the top of me. If I'm too far back, he could cow-kick me (kick forward with a hind foot).

I begin by rubbing him with my hand on the shoulder and neck. If he's relaxed, I move alongside him, rubbing him down his back and hip, and then repeat this on the other side. I rub gently, but firmly; too

66

11/ As I started to rub her shoulder, she tried to leap back. You can see how I used my right hand to push myself away.

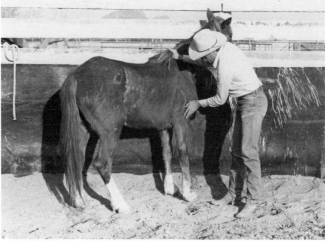

12/ After she relaxed, I resumed rubbing her . . .

13/ . . . and was able to pick up this foot for just a few seconds.

14/ I moved to the back leg and repeated the entire procedure.

15/ She stood quietly until I asked her to pick up this foot . . .

16/ . . . and she lashed out. You can tell by her expression, however, that she isn't as upset as she was in photo #11.

1/ This mare is relatively gentle, even though she hasn't been handled much. Nonetheless, I still approach her at the shoulder, the "safety position," to begin rubbing her.

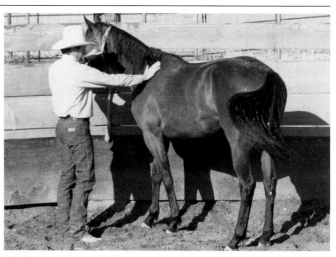

2/ I begin rubbing her on the shoulder . . .

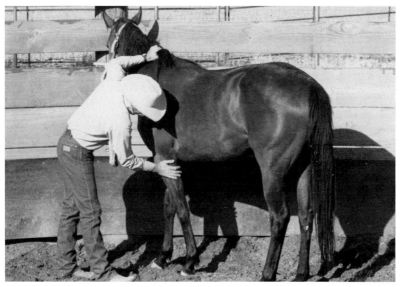

3/ . . . and move down her leg. I asked her to pick up her foot, and she responded willingly, but we won't show picking up her feet, since the first sequence was devoted to that subject.

light of a touch can make him uncertain about what I'm doing.

I will also rub him around his head and ears. The first few times, I may not actually be able to handle the ears, but I'll chip away at it a little at a time, getting closer and closer, until I can finally rub his face from the nose up to his poll . . . and then stroke each ear gently. I do this now, while sacking him out, so that when I go to bridle him, he's not head-shy or ear-shy.

I check his mouth at this same time to see if he has any wolf teeth that need to be removed, or other tooth problems. If so, I have the veterinarian do that before I bridle the colt for the first time.

When the colt will let me rub him all

over his body, I begin working with him so he will allow me to pick up his feet. I believe this should be done when sacking out a colt so he will allow the horseshoer to handle his feet. Sometimes people wait and let the horseshoer do this training, but this can backfire. If the shoer is in a hurry and a little short-tempered, he might get too aggressive with the colt. This could cause the colt to be bad to trim and shoe for the rest of his life.

Besides, it isn't the horseshoer's responsibility to train the horse. If I'm breaking him, it's my job; or it's the owner's job. It's the same way with the veterinarian. If I don't have this colt easy and safe for the vet to handle, and the vet has to get a little rough with him because he's in a hurry, the result could be a horse that's bad to doctor.

To get the colt accustomed to having his feet handled, I start with a front leg. I use one hand to rub the leg while I keep my other hand on the shoulder. That serves as my early warning system; I can feel if the colt is getting nervous and is about to jump into me. If he does, I can use that hand to push myself away from him. It's a safety factor.

First, I rub only from the shoulder to the knee. When the colt relaxes and accepts that, I move on down the cannon bone to the fetlock and pastern. If he accepts that, I ask him to pick up the foot. I pull gently on the fetlock, at the same time pushing him just slightly on the shoulder. This causes him to shift his weight a little to the other side, making it easier to pick up the foot.

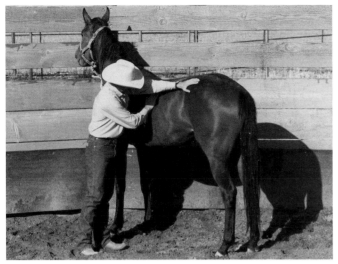

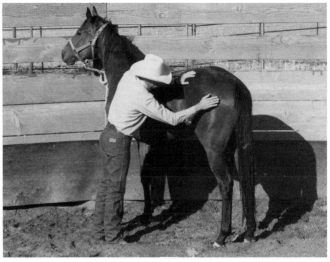

4 & 5/ I continue rubbing my way down her back to her hip.

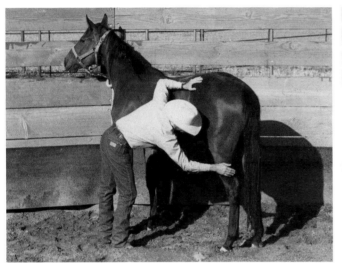

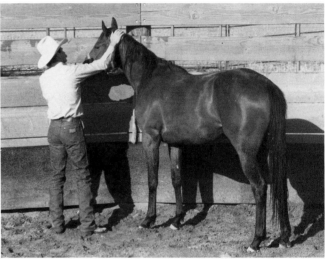

6/ I rubbed her back leg, and picked up the foot briefly.

7/ Moving back to her head, I rubbed her around the poll . . .

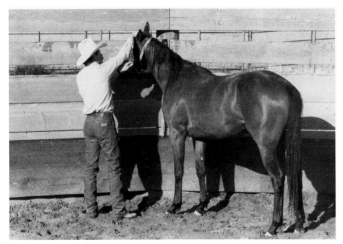

8/ . . . and on her forehead.

9/ I walked behind her, staying well out of kicking range.

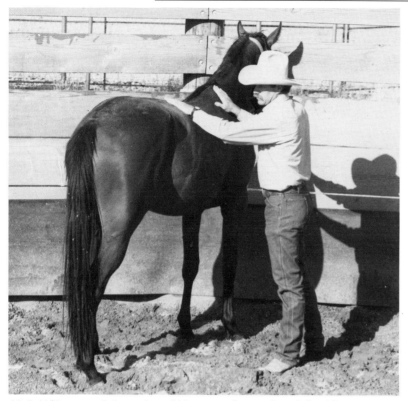

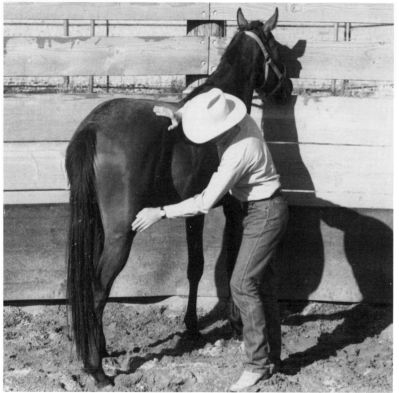

10 & 11/ I repeated the entire rubbing procedure on her right side.

If he picks it up just one inch, I'll hold it a second and immediately put it down, then relax a minute. This is where a lot of people get into trouble. The first time they ask a horse to pick up a foot, they want to hold it for 3 or 4 minutes. The horse isn't accustomed to this, doesn't like it, and tries to jerk his foot away.

This is a good example of how a person can create a problem. You can minimize upsetting him by holding the foot up just a few seconds, then it won't be as big a deal to him. Over a period of days, by gradually increasing how high you raise the foot and how long you hold it, it becomes no big deal at all. Soon he will willingly let you pick up and hold each foot with no fuss. Eventually you can even tap each foot with a hammer, and maybe drag a rasp across it once or twice to get him ready for the horseshoer.

I repeat this same procedure with all four feet. When I'm working with a back foot, I keep one hand on the hip. If I think he might kick, I don't grasp the fetlock to pick up the foot. Instead, I'll grasp the leg between the fetlock and the hock and pull it toward me—as I push on the hip, with my other hand, to take some weight off that foot. As soon as he raises the foot just an inch or two, I give it right back to him.

If he does kick, I try to hang on to the leg, and then put it down as soon as he stops. If he kicks it out of my hand, I move out of the way. When it's back on the ground again, I pick it up once more. After a while, he'll realize there's no reason to be kicking, and he'll quit. Remember: Don't hold the foot too long, and put it down before he gets tired and tries to put it down.

Whenever I pick up a back foot on any horse, I'll always start by running my hand down from the hip to the fetlock so he knows what I'm doing. If I were to grab the fetlock without any warning, it could startle him and cause him to kick. Always let the horse, and especially a colt, know where you are and what you are doing.

Sometimes on colts that have a tendency to kick, I will use a short, soft rope around the back legs so I can stay out of range. I will slip the rope around the leg up high, then let it slide down around the ankle. I will now follow the same procedure. With one hand on the hip and the other on the rope, I pick the foot up just a little, then let it down. If he kicks, he can

70

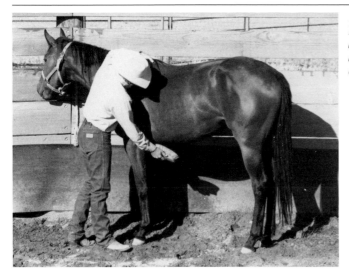

12/ Then I brushed her all over her body, and paid particular attention to the cinch area.

only kick the rope out of my hand.

If you can't get the rope around your colt's back legs, he probably isn't ready yet and needs to be gentled more by being rubbed with your hand.

After the colt will let me rub him all over with my hands, and I've picked up each foot briefly, I'll begin introducing objects to him. Usually this is on the first day, but sometimes the second or third, if the colt has never been handled much and is still a little wary of what's happening.

Generally, I start with a brush. It's not much bigger than my hand, and it feels good to a horse. I'll brush him all over his body, using firm strokes on his neck, back, and hindquarters, and being more gentle on sensitive areas like his face. I always rub and brush in the cinch area, too, to get the colt used to the feel of something being there.

The cinch area can be very ticklish, and this is why some colts react so violently (bucking or falling down) when cinched up the first time. All too often we neglect this area. But you can minimize a colt's reaction by doing your homework and desensitizing the cinch area.

I have found that some horses, especially halter horses, have been brushed on so much that their sides have been desensitized. When I get on them and go to ride them off, they ignore my legs.

After using the brush, I usually go to a saddle blanket, but you can use a gunny sack or a rag. I put it on his back initially, then slide it up his neck, down his neck and back, over his hips, then put it back on him again. I'm doing it gently and showing him there is nothing to be afraid of, and I do it on both sides of the horse.

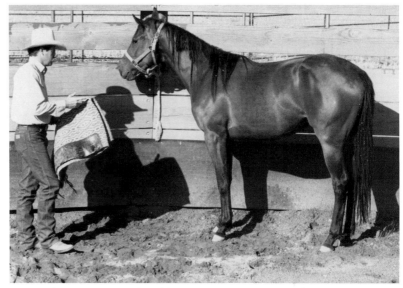

13 & 14/ Finally, I introduced her to a saddle blanket, and moved it back and forth.

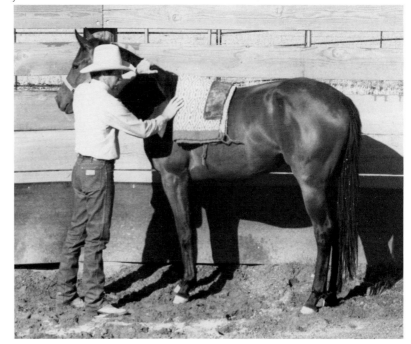

1/ Here's a sequence of my sacking out the roan gelding, who has not been handled much and is more broncy than the previous mare. While I curry him, I hold his halter so I can feel when he's going to jump.

2/ After currying him on both sides, I introduce him to the saddle blanket.

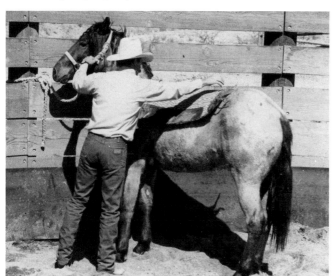

3 & 4/ I move it back and forth, and down off his rump.

You've got to work on both sides equally. Everyone has a tendency to work just on the near (left) side, but you've got to "train" both sides.

The entire time I'm working with the colt, I keep an eye on him to see what he is doing, and how he is reacting. Everything he does tells me what he is thinking and how he is going to react. Even if he is standing quietly, that tells me something—that he's relaxed and not objecting to anything I do.

However, there are some horses that stand *too* quietly. They will be like a statue—stiff, rigid, not moving a muscle. They don't even blink. These horses worry me ten times more than a nervous colt because they are time bombs waiting to explode.

They are not moving because they are too scared to move. If you keep working with them, they will finally blow, and it will be fast and wild.

When I'm working with a horse like this, I will back off and let him relax. When I see him starting to soften and relax, then I start working with him again.

If an average colt is a little afraid or nervous, I work on whatever I am doing a little longer. I'm building a foundation, and if I don't have a darn good one, everything I do later on will be built on shaky ground.

When I'm sacking out, I like to work by myself. Then I don't have to worry about anybody else's safety. If I have a helper

5/ *He tolerated it for a few minutes, then couldn't handle it any longer.*   6/ *I stood back until he quieted down.*

7 & 8/ *Then I stood on his right side and rubbed the blanket back and forth on him.*

holding the horse and he's standing on the other side of the horse from me, or even in front of him, something I do might startle the horse and he'll jump on my assistant. Or, the horse might spook from him and slam into me.

If I'm working by myself and the horse is startled, not having someone on the other side of him gives him a place to go—instead of coming in my direction. I never want a horse to jump on me.

This covers about all of the sacking out I do before I saddle a colt for the first time. However, I feel that the sacking-out process should continue as long as a colt's learning continues. By this I mean that I continually and gradually introduce him to things any well-broke horse should be acquainted with and accept, such as ropes,

slickers, crossing streams, etc., which we will cover in a later chapter.

The better a colt is sacked out before you get on, the better he is going to ride off. If a colt is a little broncy, spend extra time with him doing ground work. It will make your first ride go a lot better.

8 FIRST SADDLING

If you did a good job of sacking out the colt, the weight of the saddle should not bother him.

WHY: Unless you're going to ride bareback, you need a saddle on your horse.

HOW: Introduce the saddle to him quietly, ease it on, and cinch it up slowly.

PROBLEMS: Scaring him with the saddle; cinching up too fast and too tight.

ONCE THE colt will stand quietly while I brush him and rub the saddle blanket all over him, I introduce the saddle to him. This is just a continuation of sacking him out. If he seems curious about it when I approach him, I will let him sniff it, but generally I just go ahead and put it on him.

Usually I lay the right stirrup and cinches across the seat of the saddle before I lift it on him. That way, they won't bump against the colt on his off (right) side and scare him.

However, if I have a real bad horse that I'm saddling, I won't do that because if the stirrup did fall down, it would *really* scare him. I'll still lay the cinches across the saddle; because of their length, they are not as apt to fall. But I'll just let the stirrup hang down as I lift the saddle up. Even if the stirrup does bump him, it won't be as scary as it would be if it fell and banged

1/ When I'm ready to saddle, I lay the cinches, breast collar, and stirrup across the seat.

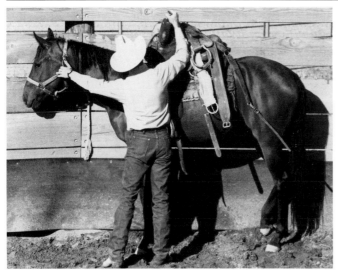

2/ *I ease the saddle up quietly and quickly. I like to use a light-weight saddle that I can easily lift with one hand for the first few saddlings. Then I can hold the halter with the other hand.*

3/ *If a colt is gentle, I can walk around to the other side to lower the stirrup and cinches, or drop them from the near side, as I'm starting to do here.*

4/ *If a colt were nervous or spooky, I would stay on his near side, and lower the stirrup with the latigo . . . and then do the same thing with the cinches. Here, I've run the latigo through the cinch rings.*

5/ *I move them across the saddle . . .*

him on the elbow or leg.

If you ride short stirrups and are afraid your right stirrup won't stay across the saddle while you lift it, you might hook it over the saddle horn. Or, better yet, tie it down with the saddle strings or piece of rope. If you are also a little on the short and light side and your saddle is so heavy and awkward you can't lift it easily, you might borrow a lighter saddle for the first few saddlings of your colt.

To avoid scaring the colt, you need to ease the saddle up quietly and quickly. But don't move too cautiously. If you keep tip-toeing around the colt, this strange behavior will make him more nervous than if you act normally. Move in a normal, business-like manner, and put the saddle on his back.

If you did a good job of sacking out the colt, the weight of the saddle should not

bother him. What I like to do now is slide the saddle around on his back just a little—before I cinch it up. I'll also take it off, and put it back on a couple of times. Just because I get the saddle on him doesn't mean I have to cinch him up real quick.

I want him to stand quietly with the saddle being taken on and off several times. If he does move around, I'll try to hold the saddle in place so it won't fall off. But if it does, I don't make a big deal out of it. I just start over. Remember: If at any point he gets scared, back up and review, then start again with what you're doing—but go slower.

If he does move around, it's because he's uncertain or scared. Keep your cool, because getting after him will only increase his fear of being saddled. Don't make saddling a big deal if you don't want it to be a big deal. And use an old saddle if you

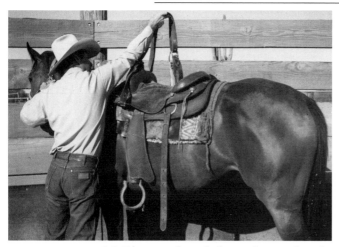 

6 & 7/ . . . and gently lower them to the other side. The breast collar is lying across the neck.

8/ I secure the front cinch first—pulling it up easily so this filly can "feel it coming." I pull it just snug enough to hold the saddle in place.

9/ I reach for the back cinch and hold it against the filly's belly so she can feel it, and I can see how she might react to it.

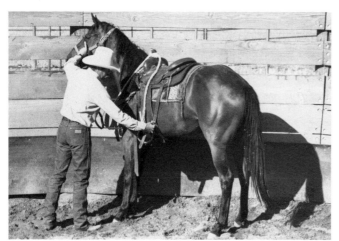 

10/ She's okay, so I go ahead and buckle it.

11/ Normally, I'll let a horse stand tied for a little while and let him get used to the feel of the saddle. I want him to learn to relax with it. But this filly is already so relaxed, I go ahead and untie her, secure the lead rope to the saddle horn, and snap on a longe line.

12/ Initially, I let her move on her own, getting used to the feel of the saddle and the cinches.

don't want your new one to fall off and get dirty.

If he's a pretty gentle colt and I think he will stand still, I'll walk around to the other side to lower the stirrups and cinches. But I won't do this if the colt is nervous or spooky. If he moves, the saddle will jiggle, he'll jump, and the saddle will fall off about the time I'm walking around behind him. Not only will that scare him even more, but he will have also learned that if he jumps, he can unload the saddle.

I feel that I can better control the situation if I stay on the left side of the colt and gently lower the stirrup and cinches by using my latigo, or a piece of rope. If he does jump a little, I'm in a much better position to hold the saddle in place.

While I'm doing this, the colt is still tied, but I keep my left hand on his neck on the halter, as my early warning system. This allows me to feel what he is doing, or about to do, while I watch what I'm doing. If he's nervous and is about to jump my way, I can feel it instantly and push myself away so he doesn't hit me with full force.

Because I have rubbed and brushed this horse in the cinch area, there shouldn't be any problem when I reach under him to get the cinch. But if he's not plumb gentle yet and I think he might kick at me, I'll do one of two things: Make a loop in my latigo to flip under him and catch the cinch, or I'll use a little hook made out of baling wire.

If your colt is still ticklish or sensitive in

13/ When I ask her to trot, she humps up a little bit. I like a longe line on a colt so if he really does buck and start running blindly, I can slow him down and get him under control. A colt can't think if he's running out of fear.

14/ This filly settled right down, and trotted and loped in both directions with no problems.

77

1/ Here's another sequence of the roan gelding—with whom I deliberately did not take time to properly prepare for the first saddling; I wanted to show what can happen when this time is not taken. Even though I did get him saddled, you can see that he did not accept it well. He's eyeballing the saddle here.

2/ I lift the saddle on . . .

3/ . . . and drop the cinches and stirrup with the latigo.

the cinch area, you should spend a little more time getting him over this before you put the saddle on him. Many colts aren't used to anything touching them there and it bothers them. If you abruptly introduce the cinch to them, it surprises them and they might throw a fit. So spend more time rubbing and brushing your colt in the cinch area when you are sacking him out.

When I'm ready to pull the cinch up, I do it easily so the colt can "feel it coming." If you pull it up suddenly, it might scare him and he'll blow up. Do that several times in a row and you have started a

bad habit that's going to be a problem to fix.

I pull the cinch just snug enough to hold the saddle in place, without cutting the colt in two. I always have a back cinch on my saddle, but before I buckle it, I lift it up against his belly to see how he's going to react to it. I don't want to surprise him with it.

Here again, if I did a good job of brushing and rubbing this colt under the belly, the feel of the back cinch won't bother him, so I go ahead and buckle it. I don't want it tight, but I do want it right against his belly and not hanging down

78

4/ I reach for the front cinch and lace the latigo through the ring.

5/ He pulls back when he realizes he is cinched up.

6/ After he settles down, I rub his belly; I had not taken the time to do this before, so I have to do it now. Then, I hold the back cinch against his belly.

7/ But as soon as I fasten the back cinch, he pulls back again. I let him stand tied about 15 minutes after this.

five or six inches. That's just a wreck looking for a place to happen since it's conceivable he could stick a back foot through it—either now, or later when I'm riding him.

Now I'll grab the saddle horn and move the saddle around on his back. Then I'll take the stirrup leathers and move them a little, gradually building up to popping the leathers together, making noise.

After this, I'll just let the colt stand there, tied to the post, and let him get used to the feel of being saddled. I want him to wear it and learn to relax with it, so that every time I saddle him from now on, he'll think there's nothing to it.

When the colt has relaxed, I untie him, snap a longe line to his halter, and let him wander around on his own so he can get used to the saddle while moving at his own speed and direction. If he bucks, I let him; but if starts running blindly, I'll slow him down with the longe line. He will

eventually see that he can't run away from the saddle, but if he's running crazy, he could hurt himself before he finds this out. The colt will be able to think better if things are going slower.

After the colt seems relaxed, I'll go ahead and longe him, asking him to trot and lope in both directions, and stop. Even though he has been introduced to something new—the saddle—he must still respond to the other cues which he has already been taught.

1/ After the colt seemed to relax a little while standing tied, I snapped on a longe line and let him move off on his own. Because I had not longed this colt before, and he doesn't understand the verbal command whoa, I don't have much control over him and can only let him buck.

2/ When he stops bucking, he looks like he might head toward me . . . so I chouse him and he heads the other way.

3/ He starts bucking again.

4/ Because the colt does not know how to longe, he keeps switching directions— and at one point gets tangled in the longe line.

5/ *I had to turn loose of the longe line when he got tangled in it . . . and he tries to jump out of the pen, but doesn't clear the fence. None of this would have happened if I had taken the proper steps, and a lot more time, in preparing the colt for being saddled.*

6/ *The colt was not hurt; he finally settled down, and trotted and loped without bucking.*

9 INTRODUCTION TO THE BIT

Teaching the horse to respond to the bit is like almost everything else we teach him: We teach him to move away from pressure.

WHY: Let colt get acquainted with the feel of the bit and how to respond before you drive him.

HOW: Let him just carry it at first; later, teach him to give to lateral and vertical pressure.

PROBLEMS: Being rough; tying reins too short; not letting horse figure out how to get relief from rein pressure.

THE MOST important thing we teach a colt is to respond properly to the bit. The bit is our key to controlling him, and without control, we have a useless horse, or at the very least, a horse that is no fun to ride.

You can go anywhere—horse shows, gymkhanas, trail rides, rodeos, neighborhood arenas, and trails—and see horses with mouth problems. They sling their heads in the air, or brace against the tie-down, or duck their heads down to the chest, or won't turn right, or left, or the mouth is wide open. All of these problems result from the horse never being taught how to respond to the bit, and/or from rough hands. A colt can be beautifully trained, but ruined later by a rider who relies on strength rather than skill.

Teaching the horse to respond to the bit is like almost everything else we teach him: We teach him to move away from pressure. When we first put a halter on him, we taught him to move forward in response to pressure from the crownpiece. We taught him to back by moving away from pressure on the nosepiece. We taught him to turn when we put pressure on the side of the halter.

When we put the bit in his mouth, we want him to move away from its pressure. In this case, we want him to relax his lower jaw and drop his nose, when we put pressure on the bit.

If he has a soft, light mouth, we won't have to pull the reins very hard to put pressure on the bit. However, there is one misconception I want to mention. A lot of people think that because a colt has never carried a bit, his mouth will be soft and mellow, and he will automatically respond to the bit properly. That's not true. You have to train the mouth, because when you first put a bit in it, the horse has no idea what you want. And usually his first instinct will be to push against the pressure, instead of yielding to it.

It will be easier with some colts than others, because horses vary in their sensitivity, just as people do. Those horses that are sensitive all over their bodies will generally be sensitive in their mouths, and therefore easier to teach than so-called "cold-blooded, thick-skinned" horses. It doesn't mean, however, that the latter type of horse will always be *heavy* on the bit. He can become easy to stop and turn, but it will take more effort to develop his mouth, and obviously he will never be as light on the bit as a more sensitive horse.

The first thing I do with a colt to introduce him to the bit is to hang a bit in his mouth and let him carry it. I usually do this after I have saddled him the first time or two. I'll let him carry the bit while I longe him. I use a plain smooth snaffle, with copper in the mouthpiece. The copper helps keep the mouth wet, which will make the mouth more responsive. Not all horses need the copper, but I have it in

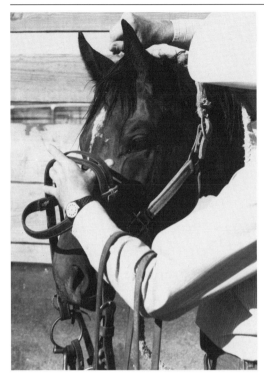

1/ I leave the halter on when bridling a colt the first few times. I lift the bridle with my left hand while reaching for it with my right.

2/ I hold the bridle with my right hand and position the bit with my left.

Usually, a colt's first instinct is to push against the pressure of the bit, instead of yielding to it.

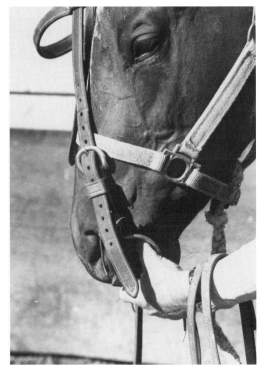

3/ I ask the filly to open her mouth by inserting my thumb into the corner of her mouth.

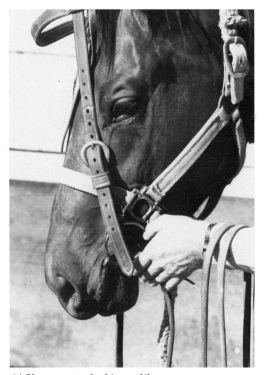

4/ She accepts the bit readily.

If I think a colt is going to be real light or tender-mouthed, I'll use a rubber snaffle.

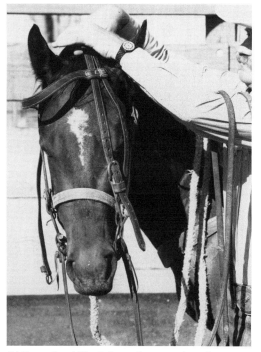

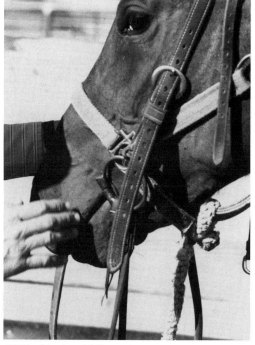

5/ Care should be taken when putting the ears through the bridle. Fold each ear forward, and gently lift the bridle over the ear. Do not poke or stuff the ear through.

6/ The bit should fit so there is just a slight wrinkle in the corners of the mouth. I'll secure the long strap so it does not flop and irritate the filly.

all my bits because it doesn't hurt to have it there.

If I think a colt is going to be real light or tender-mouthed, I'll use a rubber snaffle. It's softer, and because it's also bigger in diameter, it doesn't concentrate as much pressure in a small area as a regular snaffle does.

The first few times I bridle the colt, I leave the halter on, for control, and put the bridle over the halter. I adjust the bridle so the snaffle puts just a slight wrinkle in the corners of the mouth. But if the colt starts putting his tongue over the bit too much, I will adjust it a little higher. That makes it harder for him to roll his tongue around and maybe get it over the bit—a bad habit because then the bit lies directly on the bars of the mouth. That's an uncomfortable position and can really hurt when pressure is put on the bit.

Doing this for just a few days is usually enough, but some colts have busier mouths than others and I'll have to do it longer. If a colt continually gets his tongue over the snaffle, I'll tie the bit up in his mouth. I'll take a piece of strong string or twine, loop it around the middle of the snaffle, then bring one end out of each corner of his mouth, and tie it off to the browband or forelock.

I never put a bridle on a colt and leave it

on him all day while he's in the stall or corral. I think that's a bad practice for several reasons. First, he might catch the bridle on something and end up getting hurt, or tearing up my bridle. Second, it can interfere with the colt's chewing, and that can cause a problem. And third, he has too much time to worry about the bit and try to figure a way to get rid of it, like rubbing the headstall off.

I like to let a colt pack the bit while I'm working with him. That way, he will be paying more attention to what I'm doing and won't be thinking about the bit. Before long he will accept it, just as he does the halter or saddle.

After the colt has carried the bit a few days, I begin teaching him how to respond to it while I'm still on the ground. I want him to respond to the bit just as lightly as he does to the halter, and I believe in starting this before I drive him, or tie his head around to the side. First, I want to give him an idea of what the pressure is like from a lateral pull.

While I'm standing beside him, I'll take the rein on that side and pull it toward me, just a little bit. This gives him the idea of following the pull on the bit. If you pull real easy, and let him see just how easy it is to give to the pressure, he won't fight against it. If he does, he won't scare him-

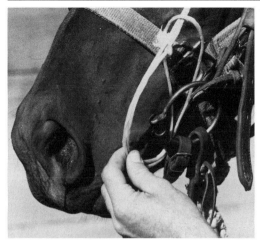

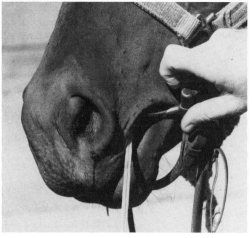

If a colt continually gets his tongue over the snaffle, I'll tie the bit up in his mouth.

1/ Here are four pictures showing how I tie up a snaffle if a colt likes to get his tongue over it. I take a piece of baling twine, or something similar, and loop it over the mouthpiece, as shown.

2/ I slide the twine to the middle of the bit.

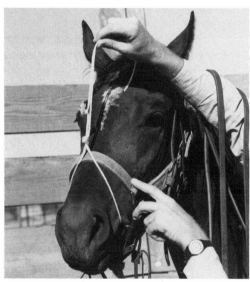

3/ I bring the two strands out of the corners of the mouth.

4/ After tying a knot in the center, I tie the two strands to the browband.

After the filly is bridled, I tie the reins to the saddle horn with plenty of slack in them. Then I longe the filly while she gets used to the feel of the bit. I might do this for several days while I'm working with the young horse.

I like to let a colt pack the bit while I'm working with him.

After the filly has carried the bit awhile, I begin teaching her how to respond to a lateral pull.

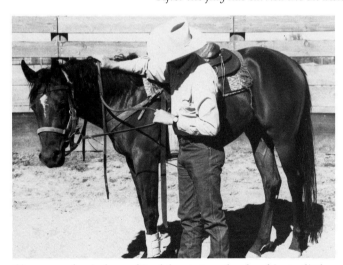

She responds nicely, and I ask her to turn her head just a little more.

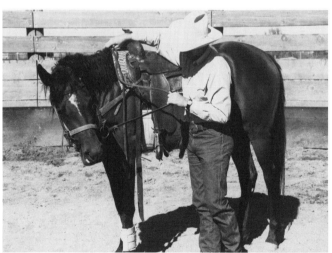

This is as far as I'll ask her to turn her head at this stage.

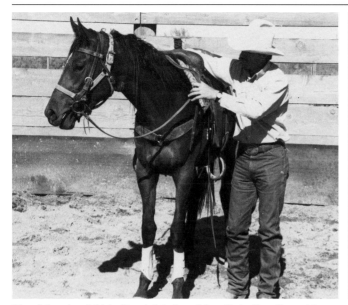

To ask her to yield to the right, I could walk to the other side . . . or use the right rein, as I'm doing here.

She gives nicely . . . and begins walking to "follow her head." This is okay.

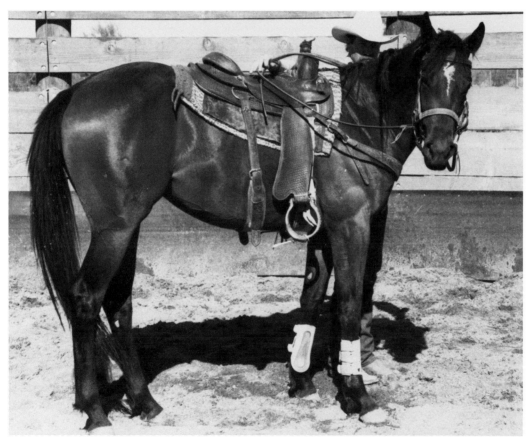

This is about as far as I want her to yield her head.

Here's how I tie off the rein that won't be used.

self as he would if he were tied solid. Once the colt understands how to get relief—simply by turning his head in the direction of the pull—then I will tie his head around to the side.

For this, I always use a piece of rubber inner tube that is attached to the back-cinch D-ring on my saddle. I don't like to use a rein because it has no *give*. When the horse tries to straighten his head out, he'll hit the end of the rein with his mouth. Not only can that scare him, but he could hurt his mouth. I want to develop the mouth so it's as light as possible, and it won't be light if it keeps getting hurt. With the inner tube, the horse can stretch without hitting

After the filly under-stands how to give to the pressure of a lateral pull, I like to use a piece of cotton rope with a snap to tie her head around. The rope is attached to a piece of inner tube secured to the back-cinch D-ring. The snap should reach just to the point of the shoulder.

I pull the nose into position with the halter (not the bit), and snap the rope to the snaffle.

The filly can stretch
the inner tube without
hitting her mouth
hard. Yet it teaches her
to give and follow the
pull. After her head has
been tied around for
maybe 10 minutes in
this direction, I'll tie it
around on the other
side.

his mouth hard. Yet it will teach him to give and follow the pull.

When I tie a colt's head around, I never leave him too long, just long enough so he has the idea and is giving. This is consistent with everything else we do with him; as soon as he understands something, give him a reward and quit asking him. Relieve the pressure.

Leaving a colt's head tied around for 2 or 3 hours will certainly give him the idea of what we want. But because he never gets any reward, he might get just plain mad, and sour out on the whole idea. Then the next time you ask him to give his head to the side, he might think, "The heck with this," and fight it. So I'd rather do it for just 10, 15 minutes, whatever it takes, watch him, and make sure he gets his reward.

If the colt is going to be a western or English show horse, I may bit him up vertically. To do this, I will run both reins back to the saddle and tie them. How snug to have the reins depends on how the horse is built, which, in turn, determines how easily he can flex. If he has a short, thick neck, especially in the throatlatch area, he might not be able to flex easily. In fact, it might not be physically possible for him to carry his head in the vertical position.

On the other hand, a horse with a long, thin neck can flex easily. But I don't want

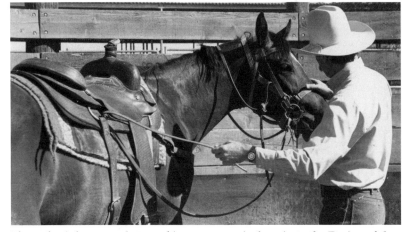

If you don't have any inner tubing, you can tie the rein to the D-ring of the back cinch. Run the rein through the D-ring, then pull the nose around with your other hand.

When the head is turned to the desired position, tie off the rein. Note how the other rein is looped over the neck and tied to the halter to keep it out of the way.

After a colt has learned to yield to a lateral pull, I may bit him up vertically. I run the reins through the front D-ring, make sure they are both the same length, and tie them off with a square knot. Here, the filly is bracing against the bit with her lower jaw.

to crank his head to the desired position the first few times I bit him up. While he's standing still, I'll take the slack out of the reins just enough so that when he moves, he'll bump his mouth if he sticks his head too far beyond the vertical.

I'll watch him trot and lope around and, if I see there's still too much slack in the reins, I'll stop him and tie them a little shorter. But I do this over a period of days. Like everything else, he has to learn this gradually. Then he won't resent it like he would if I cranked his head way down and said, "Well, you gotta learn. This is where your head should be, so I'm gonna start you this way."

I like the colt to be longeing while he's bitted up like this. One reason: He's exercising, getting the fresh out of his system, while at the same time learning how to stay off the bit. Also, when he's moving, he'll learn more quickly to give to the pull of the bit.

When a colt is standing still, he can

brace against the bit a lot easier than when he's moving. He could even develop the bad habit of bringing his chin back against his chest and getting behind the bit . . . so that he feels no pressure from it at all. If he's allowed to continue doing this, it becomes a bad habit and he will be very difficult to control when you start riding him.

Some people make the mistake of tying the reins too short. Then because the colt gets no relief when he flexes and drops his nose, he might bull up and get mad. His mouth can also become so numb and insensitive that he will not even feel the pressure when you take hold of the reins. You have created a dead mouth, one with no feel. He could also develop the habit of bringing his jaw back against his chest, here again getting behind the bit.

Once the colt learns to give to the bit easily, he's ready to drive.

Some people make the mistake of tying the reins too short.

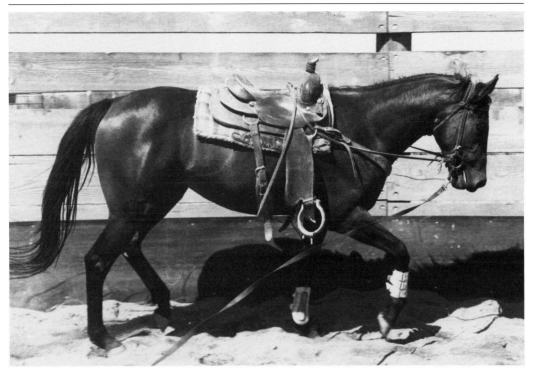

Now she's softening a little.

And here she's over-flexed. But I don't worry about this in the initial stages. I primarily want her to learn to give to the pressure of the bit, which she is doing. Once she learns, then I can show her where to correctly carry her head.

10 DRIVING

Driving gives you good control of a colt when you later mount up the first time.

WHAT: Controlling speed and direction from the ground.

WHY: For control when you get on; makes him bridlewise.

HOW: Prepare by tying head around; use surcingle or saddle, light lines; rubber bit or halter for light mouth; stay behind him; emphasize whoa, backing, turning away from you in figure-eights.

PROBLEMS: Kicking or spooking at lines; won't move forward; won't back up; spooks and starts running; won't turn.

TO MY way of thinking, driving is a very important step in breaking a colt because it gives you good control of him when you mount up the first time. By driving him, you can teach him to move forward, turn, and stop. The latter is extremely important, of course.

Before I actually drive this filly, I want her to get used to the feel of the driving lines— actually, two longe lines. Because the filly knows how to respond to a lateral pull, it's easy to drive her with the lines snapped to the halter. Here, the right line is snapped to the halter ring, run through the stirrup, and over the saddle.

If you get on a colt that hasn't had this training and he starts running or bucking, you can get into awful trouble. It's like being in a car with no brakes or steering.

Even though we have already done a swell job of sacking this colt out, we've got to let him get used to the driving lines dangling over his rump and around his hocks before we actually drive him. Therefore I actually longe him at first, with the lines snapped to the halter, one on each side. I bring the inside line straight to my hand. I run the opposite through the stirrup and over the saddle. As I let him move off, I let it slide back over his rump.

If that line doesn't bother him, I proceed to longe him, and let him get used to its feel while he's moving. Then I stop and reverse him, and let him get used to the other line flipping around his hocks.

If the lines do upset him, and he gets to thrashing around or kicking, he won't be tearing up his mouth because the lines are attached to the halter. This also gives me much better control of him without having to pull on his mouth. Until the horse stops throwing fits, I just continue to longe him.

While I'm working the horse, I try to not let the outside line drop below his hocks. If that happens, there's more of a chance that he'll get tangled up in it. If the horse ever does get tangled up, I drop the lines and turn him loose. My pulling on them just applies more pressure, which makes him fight even harder. He will eventually stop, and then I untangle him and start over.

It doesn't take most horses very long to get used to the lines. Then I snap them to the bit. But I don't run either one through the stirrups yet. Initially, I handle them just as I did when they were snapped to the halter. I'll stand in the middle of the pen and ask the horse to longe around me.

I'll ask him to stop a couple times with the direct lines. When I can see that he's going to stop and that he's not worried about his mouth, I'll run both lines through the stirrups (after tying them together) and actually go to driving him.

I start just as if I were longeing him. I position him parallel to the fence, cluck, and let him travel around the pen. Although I stay more or less in the center of the pen, I have to do a lot more walking than if I were longeing him. I let him make a couple of circles, then slowly ask him to

As I ask the filly to move off, I let the right line slide back over her rump. The left line is snapped to the halter, and comes straight to my hand. If the filly were to get upset, she won't hurt her mouth, since the lines are snapped to the halter.

Because this filly was so thoroughly sacked out, the feel of the outside line doesn't bother her as I let it slip down to her hocks. Letting it get below her hocks could result in her getting tangled in it.

Here, I'm asking the filly to stop. I stop her the same way I did when longeing her—by stepping toward the front of her head and saying whoa. She wants to turn toward me a little, so I pull on the right line to keep her straight.

93

If the horse ever does get tangled up, I drop the lines and turn him loose.

She has almost stopped. Again, the feel of the right line doesn't bother her.

Now I've got the lines attached to the bit, but they are not run through the stirrups. I'll ask the filly to stop a couple more times. When I'm sure she's going to stop, and that she's not worried about her mouth, then I'll run them through the stirrups.

With the lines now run through the stirrups, I ask the filly to stop—and she responds well.

I cluck to her, and she moves out again. I don't like to do very much driving with the lines through the stirrups because it can get the head down too low.

A surcingle is better than a saddle for driving because the lines are higher. The leather reins are run through one set of rings and tied off with a lot of slack in them. The driving lines are run through the other set of rings. This surcingle has a knot tied in it to take up some of the slack; the knot won't bother a horse for the short time I use the surcingle.

Because this filly had been longed, and then driven with the saddle, she moves off easily.

I ask her to reverse by turning her toward the fence.

stop. I let him stand there a minute, then cluck and ask him to move on.

Hopefully your horse will be a little tired so he's content to walk quietly, or maybe jog. You want to keep things controlled. If he's too fresh, however, and going too fast, forget the driving and longe him until he's ready to settle down.

After I've asked him to stop a couple of times, I reverse him while he's walking, and I turn him away from me, toward the fence. This is where having tied his head around earlier should pay off; he knows how to follow the pull of the line and turn. I take a nice light, but steady pull on the line, ease him around, and let him turn. It he fights it, I don't fight him by pulling harder, as that will make things worse. I just keep a light, steady pull on the rein. If he stops, I cluck to him and make him move; he can't turn if he's standing still.

As he turns, it's important to take up the slack in the direction in which he's turning, and feed a lot of slack to the other line. Not giving him enough slack in the outside line will confuse him.

While he's going in the other direction, I'll ask him to start and stop a few times. Then I'll reverse him again into the fence. Once he's gotten the hang of turning, I move behind him and guide him through some figure-eights in the middle of the pen.

Before the session is over, I'll ask the

Having taught her how to respond to the bit before asking her to drive pays off now.

Reversing the other way.

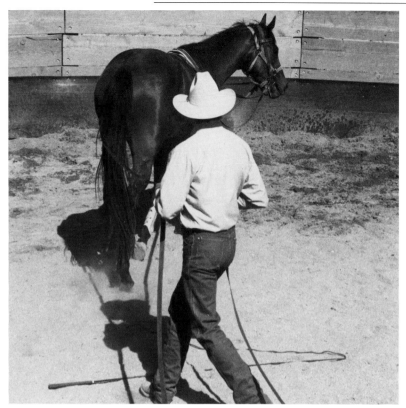

She comes around nicely.

horse to back up. I apply pressure on both lines until the horse takes a little step back. Anytime he responds to pressure, I give him slack as his reward. Then I'll ask him for another step back.

If your horse won't move, cluck to him. Clucking is your accelerator; it means the horse should go somewhere. If there's slack in the lines, he can go forward. If there's pressure on them, that's telling him to move backwards.

What should you do if your horse won't back up while you are driving him? First, review backing him while leading him with the halter until he backs easily with a light touch. Then with both halter and bridle on, stand beside him with the halter rope in one hand and the bridle reins in the other, ask him to back up easy with the reins, and if he doesn't move, use the halter to show him what you want. The horse will soon learn that pulling back on either the halter or the reins means the same thing: to back up.

What I like to do is pull on one line a little harder than the other. That makes it more difficult for the horse to lean on the bit. But you still have to pull on both lines.

I ask her to stop, and then to take a step or two back, which she does.

If you pull on just one, he'll turn around. By pulling on both lines, but one a little harder than the other, you'll keep him basically straight, but off balance, and he will have to take a step back.

Even if I think he accidentally took one step back, I'll still give him slack. After I repeat this several times, he'll realize that when he feels pressure on his mouth and hears me cluck, he's supposed to take a step back.

Over a period of several days, I try to get the colt to turn and back up in response to lighter and lighter pressure. If I had to use 2 pounds of pressure initially, I don't want to always have to use that much pressure. I would like to think that as this horse learns, he'll realize, "Oh yeah . . . that's what I'm supposed to do," and start turning or backing as soon as I start giving him the cue. And the cue should get lighter all the time.

If you don't have a surcingle, you can tie a couple of rings into your saddle, as shown here, and run the lines through them. With the lines in this position, you won't be pulling the head down as when the lines are run through the stirrups.

Driving the filly at the lope, with the lines run through the rings on the saddle.

11 FIRST RIDE

If you have taken all the steps we have detailed so far, the first ride is no big deal.

WHAT: D-Day.

WHY: Got to start sometime.

HOW: Take the edge off him first. Step on a little at a time; step on and off several times. Move around on top of him. Let him go wherever he wants to go. Relax, and let him relax.

PROBLEMS: Colt gets frightened; he won't move; he won't stop; he bucks; you can't get on him; you can't get off him; you can't steer him.

MANY people think the first ride is a case of separating the men from the boys, or separating the trainers from the bronc riders. But it doesn't have to be a rodeo. If you have taken all the steps we have detailed in the preceding chapters, and if your colt can do all of those things, then getting on and riding him off is just the next step in his training. It's no big deal, and you won't have to change from a pleasure saddle to a bronc saddle.

1/ When I'm ready to mount, I step up and down several times, getting the filly used to my weight in the stirrup. I hold the halter with my left hand; if she starts to move, I can pull her around in a circle, making it easier to either step down or swing my right leg over.

Everything we have done up to this point is preparation for the horse to be ridden. The entire time we have been working him, we have been setting him up for this next step. Horses progress through school just the way youngsters do. Kids can't go to the sixth grade if they can't pass fifth grade. While they are in fifth grade, they study what they need to know in order to pass the tests that will promote them to sixth grade.

For your colt to pass from ground work to being ridden, he must be able to do all the lessons we have talked about. The *test* will be the first time you step up on him. If you have problems, get off and repeat the lessons that will give you the control you need—or that will overcome any other problem you are having.

Let's review what you've done. The colt has been carrying the saddle and is not afraid of it. You have been driving him and he is easy to stop, turn, and back up. What you have now is control of this colt. If you don't, work the colt some more from the ground until you have it.

Before actually getting on the colt, there are two more steps you can take. First, it's helpful, but not necessary, to pony (lead) the saddled colt from a well-broke horse. He will get used to being led, so that he understands this if you want someone to pony him when you get on the first time or two. It also gets him used to seeing someone above him. That's one less thing that might startle him when you get on him, if he looks back to see where you are. This isn't absolutely necessary, but it really helps the colt.

Second, practice putting weight in the left stirrup during the two or three training sessions before you actually plan to ride him. When I do this, I usually hold the left rein and the cheekpiece of the halter with my left hand. Then if the horse starts to move while I'm standing in the stirrup, or mounting, I can pull him around in a circle, making it easier for me to either step down or swing my right leg over.

But it's probably easier for the average person to take the reins in his left hand, with the left rein a little shorter than the right. Put that hand on top of the mane. Grasp the saddle horn with your right hand, and step into the stirrup. Stand in the stirrup, but don't swing your right leg over. Step down, then repeat.

Do this several times. If the colt is quiet,

2/ When I swing my right leg over, I'm careful to not let it drag across her; that would probably scare her.

3/ I settle into the saddle.

4/ Just as I started to pick up the right stirrup, she was startled and started to walk off.

101

5/ I pull her head around with the halter to circle her until she settles down.

6/ When she does, I just let her walk off.

7/ This was actually the first time this filly had been ridden, and she's handling it well.

8/ I move my hand forward to feed her a little more slack.

then stand in the stirrup and gently pat him on the rump and along his neck. Progress until you can lean over the saddle and pat the horse on his right side. This gets the colt used to your being up there and feeling you move around and pat him; yet if he jumps, you can easily step down.

If at any point the colt gets scared or jumps, step down and work on what's causing the problem. Sometimes I just put my foot in the stirrup over and over again until the colt accepts it.

Here's a good safety tip to mention at this point: While getting on a green colt, never put your foot all the way into the stirrup. That way, if the colt jumps away from you, your foot shouldn't hang up. Not until I'm all the way on a colt, and plan to stay there do I put my feet all the way into the stirrups.

9/ With her head turned loose, she started to trot, and I just held on to the saddle horn and let her go.

10/ After she settled down and began walking again, I asked her to make a few turns toward the middle of the pen. She's responding to a very light touch.

It's a good idea to have someone around for your first ride or two. He (or she) can hold the colt while you get on, or tell you how high you flew when you came off. Even the best cowboy can have a freak accident and need help.

Although you can have someone hold the colt while you get on, I rarely do. But when I do, I have someone who's not going to leave the instant something goes wrong. You would be better off without a person like this, because you'll be counting on him to help control the situation and you could get in worse trouble waiting for his help, rather than just taking action yourself.

If someone DOES help you, he should stand on the same side of the horse you are on and hold the horse by the halter, not the bridle. Pulling on the bridle will hurt the horse's mouth and scare him even more. Since the horse accepts being controlled from the ground, the handler can stop him if anything goes wrong. Then he can lead you off or even longe you on a line until you feel comfortable enough to solo.

The last step you take before getting on the colt is to have him tired. *How* tired depends on the colt. If he's a hyper, nervous colt, you want him real tired. But even a quiet, gentle colt should be longed to get the freshness out of him so he isn't feeling real high.

After longeing him, it's a good idea to drive him a few minutes, giving him a review of everything you have taught him

11/ "Leading" her around with the rein.

so far, putting special emphasis on the *whoa* command.

Now that you are almost ready to step on him, check what's going on around you. Is the wind blowing, making him nervous? Are the dogs tied up? Is there other activity going on that might take his attention away from you? If so, wait a few minutes until things settle down. Don't jeopardize your safety, or what you have taught the colt so far. Waiting a day or two for the right conditions won't hurt any-

12/ Asking her to take a few steps back.

13/ Rewarding her with slack in the reins and a pat.

14/ To dismount, I pull her head toward me with the halter and slip my left foot almost out of the stirrup—so the toe can slip out easily if I need to step down in a hurry.

thing, and it will give you extra time to work on any rough spots in your training program.

When you are ready to get on, take the colt to the middle of the round corral. You're going to get on the same way that you have been practicing putting weight in the stirrup. Go ahead and do this a couple of times, just to make sure the colt is still accepting it. Then the next time you step up, swing your right leg over and sit down in the saddle.

Just sit there a few seconds, without putting your foot into the stirrup, and then get off. By getting on, then right off, you are actually getting away with riding your colt before he even knows it. You haven't gone anywhere, but you have gotten away with being on his back with nothing bad happening to you or him. This gives you both a boost of confidence.

Getting on the first time is the step that most people are afraid of. Even if they are inexperienced, they usually aren't nervous and don't fear getting hurt when ground-working a colt. It's getting on that first time that worries them.

But now you have done it and nothing happened, which is why we have spent all this time working the colt up to this point. Each lesson has overlapped the next, and he has advanced with gradual progress. He has accepted each new step, and he is relaxed and confident.

Now what you have is a colt that will stand quietly while you mount and dismount. Each time you get on, stay a little longer. Move around in the saddle, and rub the colt on the neck and rump so he gets used to your being up there.

He's familiar with your moving around on the ground, but it's different when you are on his back. So move around and get him used to it. The first few rides, move quietly; then as the days and weeks go by, you can move up to swinging your arm, taking a jacket on and off, and swinging a rope. But to do those things, start with something that's not going to scare him, then progress from there.

One time a man came to me with a problem. He had started his horse himself and was getting along okay, except that if he scratched his nose or waved at someone, the horse would shy. What had happened? Ever since he had first gotten on this horse, he had been afraid to move because he didn't want to scare the horse. But he forgot this one day when he saw a friend and, without thinking, stuck out his hand and waved.

Having never seen this before, the horse shied and the rider put his hand on the saddle horn to hang on, and he would leave it there the rest of the ride. The following days went about the same. Every time the rider moved his arm out too far, the horse would shy away from it. I told this fellow that if he had more friends, the horse would get over shying.

What he needed to do was let the colt see his arm stuck out to the side more. By bringing his arm back in when the colt shied, he taught the colt that if he shied, the arm would go away. Leaving the arm out there would have taught the colt that shying would not make it go away, and he would learn to accept it.

At this point your colt will let you on and off, and you can move around while on him. The next step is to let him move off at a walk, in whatever direction he wants to go. If he won't move when you cluck to him, try turning his head a little to one side. This just gets him a shade off balance so he's more likely to move.

If he still won't move, it could be that he's not sure if he should move. Don't get impatient and whack him down a hind leg with the ends of the reins. He's only doing what he thinks is right. Up to this point you have asked him to stand still while you are getting on. Now you have to show him that it's okay to move. He's more scared than unsure. Whipping him would be telling him that he has a right to be scared.

1/ Here's a sequence with the roan gelding again. My brother, George, is showing how you can get a colt used to someone above him before you get on him.

2/ Rocking the saddle back and forth to get Roanie used to the feel of it moving.

3/ With George holding the colt, I step into the stirrup a couple of times, then lean over the saddle a little.

4/ Roanie doesn't care for that, and I have to step down.

5/ This shows why it's smart not to have your foot all the way in the stirrup when mounting. Because mine wasn't, it slipped out easily.

6/ We let Roanie settle down, then tried it again. I stepped up and down a few more times, then swung my leg over.

You could do one of several things to solve this problem. If you are by yourself, get off, stand beside him, cluck to him, and ask him to move off, as you did when driving him. As he begins moving, walk alongside him, making sure you're not holding his head too tightly. Put slack in your reins.

If he's still reluctant to move out, cluck to him and then immediately tap him on the rump with the whip. Cluck, then tap; cluck, then tap—until he moves right out when you cluck, without your having to use the whip. Then get back on and cluck to him. If necessary, tap him very lightly on the rump with your whip.

If there is someone there to help you, have him lead the colt to get him started. If the colt starts, but won't keep going, let your helper longe him, at a walk. This is something the colt is familiar with and he'll soon figure out that when you cluck, he's supposed to move.

Longeing a colt on a line works real well with a rider who lacks confidence or ability. If something happens, the ground person can get the colt under control and stopped.

You could also have a good hand, who is on a good horse, pony you around the pen for a few minutes to get the colt untracked and moving. Usually this is

7/ I pick up my right stirrup.

8/ George leads me off. This is a good way to ride a colt the first time if you think he might blow the cork. But the person ponying you has got to be a good hand—mounted on a good horse.

about all it takes to let a colt know that when you cluck to him, it means to move.

Once you are on the horse and he walks off, just let him wander around a few minutes and let him get used to carrying your weight and having you on top of him. In fact, you can do nothing more than walk this first time, if that's all you want to do. Taking your horse slowly is always all right; it's going faster that will get you into trouble. You can even walk several days before you ever ask him to trot.

Always remember that you do not have to follow any set time schedule; just progress at whatever pace you feel comfortable. I know one lady who starts a colt just about the same way I do. When she starts riding him, she'll walk and trot the colt in the round pen about a half-dozen times, making sure she has control of him for turning and stopping.

Then she begins riding him outside in the pastures, at a walk and a trot, going up and down hills, crossing streams, winding through trees and around brush. She won't ask him to lope for maybe a month. By that time she is confident in her control of him, and he is so accustomed to being ridden and carrying her weight that when she legs him into a lope, he picks it up easily, and never thinks about pitching.

With the colts I break, I'll generally trot and lope them the first day, unless a particular colt is really nervous. Then I might wait a day or two. A colt is most apt to try and buck when at a lope, so if your colt is nervous and you're not sure about things, wait a few days until he relaxes.

9/ When Roanie looks like he's going to be okay, George hands me the lead rope and turns me loose. Following George's horse, however, gives Roanie the incentive to keep moving instead of stalling out.

10/ I never ride a colt for the first time like this—ESPECIALLY with my brother holding the line AND a whip! But it is a good way for a novice rider to put the first ride or two on a colt.

11 & 12/ Now Roanie and I are soloing again. I'm asking him to turn into the fence.

13/ He comes around without losing any forward motion.

14/ Turning the other way.

Even though the colt knows how to turn, I let him pick the direction he wants to go. I don't want him thinking about too many things until he's used to my being up there. At this point, I am just continuing to sack him out. I used a blanket first, then the saddle, now my body.

After he will walk off readily and is relaxed, I'll ask him to trot a little. I generally cluck to ask him to move faster because he has already learned that from being longed and driven. Because he doesn't know what leg pressure is, I could scare him if I bumped or squeezed him with my legs. But after a while, I will begin using my legs *after* I cluck, so he begins associating leg pressure with moving. But I'll do it very lightly. If he doesn't move, I'll cluck louder, or tap him with my reins on his rump.

If the colt picks up the wrong lead, I don't worry about it. If I can slow him down to a trot, and then put him back into the lope and try for the correct lead, I will. But if I would have to pull on him too hard to slow him down, I'll just leave him alone and let him lope on the wrong lead. For the first few rides, it doesn't matter.

Some colts today are so quiet, or lazy, that it's difficult to get them to stay in a lope. To keep them going, you have to "build a bigger fire," such as by whacking them with the reins. But do this with caution, because it can irritate or scare a colt and cause him to buck.

I'll still leave his head alone at the trot and lope. Since I'm in a round corral, there's nothing he can run into. There have been times when I've ridden colts for the first time and never had to pick up my reins. To stop them, I just said whoa, and they stopped.

About the only time I'll pick up the reins is to change directions, which I always do at the walk for the first ride or two. As a rule, I'll turn him into the middle of the pen, to turn around, rather than into the fence. That's because I don't want to turn him too tightly at this stage.

With all the driving you've done with your colt, this should be easy for him. But remember that all you should teach your colt on the first ride is to get used to carrying your weight, and seeing you on top of him. Before today, you have been getting the colt ready to ride. Now that you are riding him, you are getting him ready to be trained.

15 & 16/ Asking him to back with a very light pull, and getting a good response.

17/ *Encouraging him to move faster with body language—leaning forward— and clucking.*

18/ *As he moves out, I hold the saddle horn and just let him go. I know I can stop him when I want to.*

Whether my colt is walking, trotting, or loping, when I want to stop him, I'll sit down in the saddle, say whoa, and pull on the reins very lightly. As long as he slows down and eventually stops, that's fine with me for the first few days.

After we have walked, trotted, and loped (maybe) in both directions, I'll ask the colt to back up . . . unless I've gotten him too tired. If so, I'll wait until the next ride. I want to make it as easy as I can for him to back up.

Never back your colt in deep ground, such as sand or a freshly worked arena. Smooth, packed ground is the best. And never ask him to back uphill, not even on a small grade.

When I back a colt, I don't pull him back; I want him to back because I have asked him, and not because I am forcing him. I take the slack out of the reins, put a little pressure on his mouth, and wait for the colt to back away from it.

This is when you need to have a lot of *feel* in your hands and body, because you need to give him slack at any backwards movement that he makes. It might not even be a step back; he might just lean back, and at first that's okay. He's moving away from the pressure and you should release it immediately. If you hold on and wait for him to take a couple of steps, he could quit trying before you reward him, and then you haven't taught him anything.

At this point, the colt is still learning to move away from pressure. Although we have taught him to back up when driving him, he might be confused with you on his back. When you put pressure on his mouth, he might move forward, sideways, or sling his head. He doesn't remember that backing up will get rid of the pressure. Just review what you have taught him during the driving lessons.

If he moves around, maintain the same light pressure on his mouth until he, either on purpose or accidentally, leans or takes a step backwards. If he is slinging his head, you are probably pulling too hard. I like to pull just enough so that it's uncomfortable for him and he tries to move. As soon as he moves in the direction I want, I give him slack, which is his reward. I'll leave him alone for a minute, then I'll ask him again.

The second time should be easier. Obviously, the smarter a horse is, the easier he'll learn this. But even if he backs away from the bit by accident and not because he has figured it out, I'll still keep asking him in the same easy way, because he learns by repetition. Instead of moving forward or sideways, or just standing there with his feet planted, he'll find out through the process of elimination that the fastest way to get relief from the pressure is to back up. Because he learned to back when you were driving him, this will be easy.

The first day I ride a colt, I'll back him only a couple of times, which might consist of only one or two steps. The harder it is for a colt to figure out what I want, the less I'll ask of him. If he moves backwards just one step in a nice, easy manner, he won't resent being asked to do it. The next day, I can get the same reaction and try to improve on it. It's the building-block theory: Build a little each day.

At this point, I'll generally quit the colt. The first ride should be just another small step in his schooling. I want to ride him long enough that he is familiar with my being on top of him, but not long enough that he'll resent my getting on him the next day.

Since you've already stepped off your colt before, he'll remember this exercise. The important thing for you to remember is to not surprise him. Here's what I do.

First, I'll ease my left foot halfway out of the stirrup. That way if he jumps while I'm getting off, my foot won't hang up in the stirrup and he won't drag me around like a rag doll. I put both reins in my left hand, with the left rein a little shorter, and take hold of the mane with the same hand. My right hand is on the horn.

I'll shift my weight around a little to alert him that I'm up to something different. I say whoa, then swing my right leg over and onto the ground, being careful not to drag it across his rump. If the colt starts to move as I'm shifting my weight or while I'm stepping down, I pick up the reins easy, say whoa and stop him, and start over again.

Because my getting all the way on and off was a new thing the colt learned today, I'll do it three or four times before I put him up. This is another example of the colt learning through repetition. To ensure the horse remembering this lesson, I'll repeat it several times. He's a little tired and relaxed, and wanting to get along with me. When I repeat the lesson the next day, he'll accept it in the same frame of mind.

The first ride should be just another small step in his schooling.

12 THE FIRST 30 DAYS

In this preliminary stage, it is important to *teach* the colt to *learn*.

WHAT: This is the time to give your colt quiet miles, to let him relax and enjoy being ridden, and to start teaching him the different cues he'll need later. He doesn't need to respond to them fancy or fast, just willingly.

WHY: To continue building a good foundation on your colt.

HOW: Through improving his walking, trotting, and loping; teaching him to rate his speed and how to respond to leg pressure; beginning the development of his mouth; improving his stopping, and backing and circling; teaching him to pick up his leads.

PROBLEMS: The colt leans on the bit; travels too fast; shoulders in or out; drags his feet when he backs; carries his head too high or too low; is nervous or goosey; won't go to corners in the arena. Asking him to do too much too soon.

I like to give a colt lots of quiet miles, letting him relax and enjoy being ridden.

A horse that walks off while you are mounting is not only annoying, but dangerous. If you continue to let a horse do this, he will only get worse.

WE HAVE already started building a good foundation on our colt because of the time we have spent in doing the proper ground work. To continue building this foundation during the first 30 days, I like to give a colt lots of quiet miles, letting him relax and enjoy being ridden. But at the same time, I also begin quietly teaching him the basics of many things. He doesn't need to do them real fast or real fancy, just willingly.

At the end of 30 days, I want him to stand like a rock while I get on him. I want him to have a good walk, to move along at a nice trot, and to pick up the lope without charging off. I want him to lope nice, easy circles both ways, on the correct lead.

I want him to stop readily, but he doesn't have to make a hard stop. When I put my leg on him, I want him to move away from it. I don't expect him to spin, but I do want him to cross over with his front legs; and I want him to do a turn on his forehand. He should be soft and light in the mouth, and back up correctly, even if it is slow. I want to be able to drag a log or railroad tie off of him, and I want him to stand quietly while I put on a slicker. I also want to be able to take him for quiet rides outside of the arena, without his being a bundle of nerves.

You can't teach your colt to be a reining horse in 30 days, so don't try. In this preliminary stage it is important to *teach* him

1/ To correct this mare, I make her stand still as I prepare to mount, and I have the reins short enough so I can quickly check her.

to *learn.* When we ask him to do something, we want him to look for a way to do it, instead of a way to get out of it. For example, we are going to start teaching him the different cues he will need to know, but we will only give him a slight suggestion of a cue, and will set him up so it's easy for him to respond correctly.

You'll find that if you take a little more time with a colt, he will learn a lot faster,

113

2/ As soon as she takes a step, I check her with the reins to stop her.

3/ I stand in the stirrup, keeping pressure on the reins, until she stands still.

4/ Even after I have swung my leg over and settled in the saddle, I make her continue to stand. I don't let her move until I ask her to. Continually repeating this lesson will teach a horse to stand for mounting.

although it might not seem so at first. You can pull and jerk a colt around and have him doing quite a bit after just 2 weeks. But since he is being rushed, there is no foundation to his training. At the end of 30 days, whatever he can do is done out of fear, not comprehension. He will be inconsistent.

Meanwhile, you could be riding him

quietly, schooling him on the basics, making quiet circles . . . and it won't look like the colt is doing much of anything at 2 weeks. But because you are building his foundation, he will be able to do several things at the end of 30 days in a willing and relaxed manner. And he'll be much farther ahead of the colt that was rushed.

During the first 30 days, I continue sacking the colt out. I don't mean rubbing him with a sack or blanket, because he is already used to those things, but teaching him to relax and accept strange things and situations. Actually, this is an ongoing process because you can't introduce everything to a colt that he might meet up with in his lifetime. For now, I'll just work on things that will immediately help make him a better horse, such as swinging a rope on him, pulling a log, and having him stand still while I put on a slicker.

I'll also ride him out in the desert, letting him get familiar with the sights and sounds of the outdoors. This can be a real learning experience for a colt raised in a pen. I'll take him up and down hills and dirt banks, cross water, and ride him down a quiet road so he can get used to traffic.

One of my pet peeves is a horse that walks off while I'm getting on. It's not only annoying, it's dangerous. If the rider gets only halfway up when the horse starts moving, and doesn't have the strength or skill to pull himself on into the saddle, he can fall off and possibly get hurt.

With few exceptions, this bad habit is caused by the rider, and it starts innocently enough. The rider is barely in the saddle when the horse starts moving, and the rider doesn't stop him. It progresses from there—until the rider barely gets his foot in the stirrup when the horse starts moving.

The solution is to never let the habit get started. ALWAYS make your colt stand still while you mount up, get settled in the saddle, and pick up your right stirrup. Never let him start moving until you tell him to. Make sure you are not poking him with the toe of your left boot when you get on, causing him to move off.

If everything has gone according to plan, your colt should have learned to stand still before you got on for the first ride. If standing still has become a problem, back up and repeat the earlier lessons. Make him stand still while you put your foot in the stirrup to mount . . . and then after you get on. Work on that repeatedly.

Walking, Trotting, Loping

After the first few rides on your colt, you should be able to walk, trot, and possibly lope him in both directions and not have any wrecks. You have everything under control. You can turn and stop him because of the ground work you have done. During the next 30 days, we want to make all of these things more solid. One of the first things we want to accomplish is to have the colt relax while at the walk, trot, and lope. Whenever I get on a colt, I want him relaxed. You can't teach anything to a horse if he is not relaxed and thinking.

If the colt is hyper, nervous, and ready to explode with energy, there's no point in my getting on and fighting him to make him walk quietly. Instead, I'll longe him. Even if I've started riding a colt, I might continue to longe him before I get on— for 1, 2, 3 weeks, whatever it takes to settle him down.

Some horses that are broncy and have a cold back also need to be warmed up before you get on and start working them. I'll longe them for a few minutes until they get it all out of their system. When I do get

on, they are relaxed, and I can ride off and have a good training session.

If you get right on a cold-backed horse, he might hump up and pitch a little. If this happens two or three times, it could quickly become a bad habit, and horses seem to learn bad habits faster than good ones. I'm trying to instill good habits in my colts' minds that will stay with them the rest of their lives. And that's why I want to go slow the first 30 days. Because a colt is so impressionable, and because everything he is learning is new, I take the time to teach him correctly.

I like a horse to walk out, and I try to encourage a colt to move a little faster if he tends to be slow. But I don't hassle or get after him about this because I don't want to constantly nag at him. Usually after a colt learns to pack a rider's weight, he will naturally start walking out a little better, especially if you are outside of the arena and going someplace. There isn't much incentive for him to walk faster in a pen or arena.

I think trotting is very good for a young horse, and I get lots of training done at a trot. A colt should learn most things at the trot before he is asked to do them at the lope. Speed is where you get into trouble. And if a colt can't handle something at the trot, there's no way he can at the lope.

When I first get on a colt, I like to walk for a few minutes, and then trot before I ask him to lope. If I'm riding out in the desert, I might trot a half mile first. And sometimes I won't lope a colt on a particular day. If he has a lot of *go* in him and wants to charge off, letting him lope doesn't teach him to rate his speed and control his energy. Besides, I'd have to pull on him too much to keep him under control.

So I will make him trot during the entire training session. Trotting, especially a long trot, will relax a horse. And it will also tire a horse. He might start out at a pretty brisk trot, but then he will begin to tire, rate himself, and slow down. I've had some horses that had so much *go* that I'd trot them for 2 or 3 weeks, never letting them lope. If they broke into a lope, I slowed them down, put them back in a trot, and put slack in the reins again.

I like to ride horses with slack in the reins—at all three gaits. I don't like to hang onto the mouth because that dulls it. When the horse begins to lose sensitivity

If a colt is hyper, nervous, and ready to explode with energy, I'll longe him.

Trotting is very good for a young horse, and I get lots of training done at the trot.

in the mouth, you have to pull harder.

Trotting teaches the horse a good habit: to walk and trot quietly when I get on him. If he knows he's not allowed to go any faster until he relaxes, he won't get chargey and try it. I follow this procedure—walking and trotting quietly—every day to create the good habit I want: to slow down and take it easy.

When I have a lazy, lethargic horse, I will ride him a little more aggressively, but I don't get very many of those horses.

When I move a young horse into a lope, I want him to lope slowly. However, a lot of young horses have a tendency to go fast, especially when they are not yet accustomed to loping and carrying a rider. When they learn to balance themselves better, they'll usually begin to slow down.

At first, I leave a colt alone if he's loping fast. If I'm in the arena, he can't go anywhere, so I just pitch some slack in the reins and let him go. I even do the same thing riding outside in the desert, because it won't be very long until the colt will tire and start slowing down by himself.

I don't want a colt to do a little pitter-pat western pleasure lope—just a nice, easy, quiet lope. If he persists in loping too fast,

I will ride him in a confined area, like my arena, and lope him in circles. Or, if he starts building steam at the lope and I need to get things back under control, I'll bring him down to the trot. At the trot, I can control him more easily without having to pull on his mouth so much. Once he's trotting nicely, I'll put him back in the lope. I'll keep repeating this. Every time he starts going too fast, I'll bring him down to the trot. With the average colt, it won't be too long before he realizes there's no point in galloping like a race horse because I'll make him slow down to a trot.

If that doesn't work with a super-charged colt, I'll overemphasize the slow-down by asking him to stop. I won't haul on his mouth to make an abrupt stop; I'll just ease him down to a stop. Here's the procedure I follow: If he's loping too fast, I take a light hold, and if he doesn't slow down, I bring him all the way down to a stop. Then I might even back him up a step or two to impress upon him the control that I have. I put him back in a nice trot, then ask him to lope again. If he speeds up, I ease him down to a stop again.

If you do this repeatedly, the colt will begin to respond to a light touch on the reins by slowing down. This is putting what I call "rate" on the colt. You can rate his speed with just a light touch on the reins, but you must be firm and persistent

116

This colt is relaxed and quiet while loping in the arena.

to accomplish this. Doing it repeatedly one day, and then letting him gallop as fast as he wants the next day will not accomplish it.

If your colt is a real high-octane type, longe him . . . either before you get on, or when he is not responding to the reins when you ask him to slow down. Get off, take him to the round pen, and longe him. Or, turn him loose in the arena. Either remove his bridle, or tie up the reins with slack in them. When I do this, I don't put a line on the colt; I just chouse him around. Usually if he feels real good, he won't need much chousing. You always want your horse—whether he's a green-broke colt or a 10-year-old—safe to ride. If longeing him is what it takes to get him slowed down, do it as long as necessary.

My goal is to be able to lope nice, easy controlled circles on the colt; and to have him lope nice and easy when we are going straightaway across the desert. This teaches him to go someplace, and also helps him to learn to travel in straight lines.

As the colt progresses and responds nicely by slowing down when I take a light hold on the reins, I'll put even more rate on him. When he's loping too fast, I'll pick up on the reins. The instant he starts to slow down, I'll give him slack. He might speed right back up again; if he does, I'll take a hold again and ask him to slow

down. This will show him the rate of speed I want in him. Eventually he'll realize that I just want him to slow down one gear (instead of stopping), and when he does, I give him slack. Doing this consistently will create a good habit in the colt: to slow down as soon as I take hold of the reins.

Leads

A colt should learn how to pick up and travel in the correct lead during the first 30 days. I always move him into the lope from the trot because it will be some time yet before he's advanced enough to pick up the lope, much less the correct lead, from a walk.

Here's how I'll do it, whether I'm in the arena or out in the desert. I'll put the colt in a trot of medium speed. If I want him to pick up the left lead, I'll turn his nose just a little to the left, bump him with my right leg, and cluck to encourage him to go

1/ This sequence shows how I trot a horse into the left lead. Here, I'm asking the mare to trot faster.

2/ As she reaches a trot of medium speed, I tip her nose a little to the left, and bump her with my right leg.

3/ She has almost moved into a lope on the left lead. Notice where my left hand is—turning her head slightly to the left—and how my left foot is well away from her side so I don't give her conflicting signals.

faster—until he breaks into a lope.

To ask him to pick up the right lead, I'll turn his nose ever so slightly to the right, bump him with my left leg, and cluck to him. I'm careful to not pull his nose too far to the inside, as this will pull him off balance and he will pick up the wrong lead.

If you're not having any success picking up the correct lead, try trotting in a large circle. Again, be careful not to put too much arc in his body. If you are trotting to the right in a circle and pull his nose too far to the inside (to the right), it can cause him to drop his inside shoulder. Or it can cause him to drift out with his outside (left) shoulder, and pick up the left lead even though he's moving to the right.

Another method I use is to enlist the aid of a fence. Assume I want the colt to pick up the right lead. I'll trot a fairly large circle in my arena, and move toward the fence at a 45-degree angle. When we are almost at the fence, I'll turn the colt's nose very slightly to the right, bump with my left leg, and cluck to him. If I time it just right, I'll reach the fence just as I ask him to pick up the right lead; the fence will force him to move to the right, and he should pick up the lead.

One note about posting. Usually I'll post the trot, and when I ask the colt to lope, I'll sit down in the saddle because this will help drive him forward a little faster. (Posting, of course, is rising up and down in the saddle to the rhythm of the trot.)

By the end of 30 days, my colts will pick up whichever lead I ask for, from a trot, when I turn the nose slightly, sit down in the saddle, bump with my outside leg, and cluck.

On the rare occasion that a colt picks up the wrong lead, I don't make a big deal out of it. I just keep setting him up and doing the right things. He'll get better. Losing my patience and getting after him will make him afraid every time I ask him for the lope. Then he'll tense up, and the chances for him picking up the wrong lead are even greater.

Leg Pressure

As your horse learns more about leg pressure, this will help him in picking up the correct lead. With an average colt, I'll start using a little leg on him after I've ridden him maybe four or five times. With a goosey colt that's pretty body-sensitive, I'll wait longer.

However, it is important to get started with leg pressure as soon as possible because it can help you teach your colt lots of things, and it's something you will use on him the rest of his life.

When I say "leg pressure," I mean teaching a colt how to respond when I apply pressure from my legs. When I pressure him with my left leg, that means move to the right. Pressure from my right leg means move to the left. Pressure from both legs simultaneously means speed up.

I'll start using subtle leg pressure on a colt while I'm walking or trotting in circles, or going around some brush in the desert. If we are making a circle to the right, I'll lightly bump him several times with my left leg. Not my boot or spur, but with the calf of my leg. I'll do the same thing with my right leg when we are circling to the left.

It's easy to remember which leg to use if you just think of your horse as a box. If you want a box to go to the left, you push it on the right side. Pushing it on the left certainly won't make it go to the left. But it will when you want the box to go to the right.

When you are moving in a circle and you apply outside leg pressure, the horse gradually begins to associate it with the direction in which he is moving. For example, if you are circling to the right and he feels your left leg bump him once or

4/ As she breaks into a lope, I stay down in the saddle, using body English to continue driving her forward.

5/ She's starting to level out here as she continues loping in the left lead.

1/ Here's how I'll sometimes use a fence to help a horse pick up a lead. I'll trot a large circle, and then head for the fence at a 45-degree angle, as I'm doing here.

2/ I want the mare to pick up the right lead, so I'm turning her nose to the right.

3/ She's still trotting while she starts turning to the right.

4/ As the mare makes the turn, I sit down in the saddle and bump her with my left leg to ask her to lope.

5/ I am still driving her forward and asking her to lope. She is just starting to reach with her right front.

6/ She has picked up the right lead.

7/ Now she has smoothed out. At this point I don't worry about how fast she goes.

1/ *This is the starting position for side-passing.*

2/ *I want to side-pass to the right, so I am bumping her with my left leg until she takes a step. I use the reins to try to keep her front end straight.*

3/ *She is stepping with her left front and right hind. After she puts those feet down, I let her stand briefly as a reward, since this maneuver is so new to her.*

4/ *Although her body isn't straight, she is moving away from my left leg and that is my main concern. She'll learn to stay straight later.*

1/ Here's a sequence showing a side-pass to the left. The mare is crossing nicely in front.

2/ She's moving her front end well, but the rear end needs to catch up.

twice, he will begin to associate pressure from your left leg with turning right.

You do not, however, want to keep continuous pressure on him while you are circling because then he will begin to pay no attention to your leg. Just bump him two or three times when you start to circle.

To begin teaching the horse more leg, I like to use the fence. While walking, I'll head the colt straight toward the fence. When he's just a foot or two away from the fence, I'll stop him, and bump him with, let's say, my left leg. Bumping him tells him he's supposed to go somewhere. He can't go forward because of the fence; if he backs up, I'll use both legs to move him forward to the fence again. I'll use my reins to steady his head and keep him facing the fence.

He should quickly figure out that he should move right, in somewhat of a side-pass. As soon as I feel him take just one step to the right, I'll release the pressure and pat him. At this stage, I'm not worried about him making a perfect side-pass to the right. All I want now is for him to move away from my left leg. We will

3/ I've slowed down the front end, and she is crossing behind to catch up.

This colt that is farther along in his training is side-passing to his right in the desert.

This photo shows very light pressure being applied by my left leg. I try to keep leg pressure as subtle as possible.

work up to perfection over a long period of time.

When I'm bumping him with my leg, that's just what I'm doing. I do not bring my leg out 2 feet away from him and then thump him with it. Nor do I keep it on him, applying constant pressure. I just bump-bump-bump him enough to irritate him into moving away from it.

If I'm bumping him with my left leg and he tries to move into it, I keep bumping him until he moves away from it. Then it's important to instantly stop bumping him, to let him know he did what I wanted. If I

keep bumping him, asking him to take too many steps at first, he'll just get confused, not knowing what I want. Once he learns that when I bump him with my left leg he is supposed to move to the right, then I can gradually build on that.

It's logical to think that because the horse now knows to move away from your left leg, it'll be a snap to teach him to move away from your right leg. Not so. The horse will likely think that when you bumped him before, he got relief by moving to the right. So that's what he'll probably try. It will take him awhile to figure out that when you bump with your *right* leg, he is to move *left*. So don't get discouraged. Just be patient and persistent.

Don't work on this too long. When the horse takes a step to the side, ride off and do something else for a while. Then ride back to the fence and try it again. I like to get the colt responding fairly well in one direction before I ask him to go the other way; it seems to be less confusing to him this way.

Once I get him to take one or two steps both ways, I'll quit that lesson for the day. The next day, I'll work on it again, and as soon as I get one or two steps both ways, I'll quit. I think a colt learns more from quick, positive lessons than long, drawn-out lessons.

By the third or fourth lesson, I can get several steps both ways because I have built such a good foundation. Now, it's a matter of continuing to build on it. In all the training I do—in everything I ask the horse to do—my goal is to have him move away from pressure.

Eventually this will give me total control of the colt's body. The reins control the head and neck, and my legs control his shoulders, rib cage, and hindquarters. In reality, the ability to control the body with my legs also helps me to control the head and neck with my legs. If there's an alignment problem with the body, the head and neck will be affected.

Turning

Because of your ground work, the colt knows how to turn, but not very well. Now we need to improve on it, and the best way I know is to give the colt a reason to turn. That's another reason why I like to ride outside. There are lots of trees, bushes, and cactus in the desert. When I'm riding along and come to a tree and rein the horse to go around it, that's giving him a reason to turn. It's helping him around something.

Pretty soon when I pick up a rein, he'll automatically turn and go that way. That's another reason why riding outside will help accelerate your training. In the arena, when you rein him to turn, he really can't see any reason for going that way. The lesson is not as meaningful, and therefore doesn't register as quickly. Of course, you could set up some obstacles in the arena and that will help.

At this stage of training, I still have the colt in a snaffle and am direct-reining him. I won't begin neck-reining him for a while. Neck-reining too soon can get the colt to sticking his nose out to the left when you are turning him to the right, and vice-versa.

When I am ready to start a colt neck-reining, after about 30 days, I like to do it in the desert, while he's relaxed and traveling easy. I'll ride him with one hand on the reins. As I come to a bush, the colt

1/ This filly is just learning the basics of a turn-around. I have been walking her in a circle to the right—and now want her to take a big step to the inside with her right front. She's confused as to what I want, and does not do it.

2/ I ask her to walk out again.

3/ This time I got her to take that big step.

4/ As soon as I got it, I let her walk out again. I'll keep repeating this, in both directions.

already knows he's to go around it. So I'll give him a little direct rein and at the same time bring the other rein across his neck lightly. Pretty soon, when he feels just the neck rein, he knows to move away from it and go around the bush. If he gets confused, I'll help him out with the direct rein, then go back to riding with one hand. This gives him the foundation for neck-reining, and I'll improve upon it later.

During these first 30 days, I like to teach the colt the basic step for a spin. All I want him to do is learn to pick up the inside foot and move it to the inside. I don't force it on the colt, and I don't make a big deal out of it. I just sort of hint to him what I want.

I'll walk the colt in a circle. Just before I feel his inside forefoot come off the ground, I'll lift the inside rein to ask him to move that front foot farther to the inside when he puts it down. Then I'll let him walk a few more strides, and repeat it. It's a very subtle step to the inside, and requires a lot of feel and timing.

When I can feel the colt doing this at the walk, I'll ask him at the trot, and eventually at the lope. Not to turn, but just to move his inside foot farther to the inside.

This is the basic maneuver in learning to turn around (spin) faster later on; it will also help the colt improve his learning to move in the direction I am pulling, and in learning to turn. For a horse to turn correctly, whether it's in a spin, roll-back, or simple turn-around at the walk, he must start by moving his inside forefoot in the direction of the turn. Every horse needs to know this. And this little drill on a green colt is the first step. When he is solid at that, I'll ask for two steps; then after awhile, three, then four.

By the end of 30 days, I want the colt to be able to make one or two complete turnarounds from the walk. I want the rear end planted, and the horse to step around with his front end, smoothly and fluidly. I shouldn't have to pull hard, but I will help him out. I won't expect him to turn on his own.

Stopping

By the time I get on a colt for the first time, he already has a pretty good idea of what *whoa* means from the time I've spent leading, longeing, and driving him. So I seldom have any problem getting him stopped when I start riding him in the round pen. I just say whoa, sit down in the saddle, lightly pull the reins, and ease him to a stop.

With most horses that are relaxed and gentle, it's very easy to put a better stop on them. In fact, with some of them you have to keep asking them to lope because they don't really want to. As soon as you stop pedaling, they quit going. These horses are real easy to stop.

The ones we need to discuss are those that have a lot of *go.* It's real easy to get into trouble with a horse like this. He's loping and going faster than you want. You say whoa and take ahold of him, and he doesn't stop or even slow down. So then you start pulling on his face harder. Since he can pull as hard as you can, you've got big trouble.

With a horse like this, it's pointless to ask him to stop, because he's not thinking stop; it's the farthest thing from his mind. The key is to never let him get going so fast you can't control him.

As I've already mentioned, I'll longe a colt that's full of energy before I ever get on him, to let him get some of the play out of his system.

Then for that particular training session, I'll keep him at a walk and a trot. If I can't stop him from a trot, I sure as heck can't stop him from the lope. Not until the end of the session when he is a little tired and looking to stop will I ask him. And that might be 2 hours after trotting him through the desert, or however long it takes to get him tired.

When I ask a horse to stop, I sit down in the saddle. Any time I sit down or lean back, I am telling my horse that I want him to slow down and stop. It's a definite cue, just as my leaning forward means go faster. On a real good, broke horse, the minute you say whoa and sit down, he'll stop—without you ever having to pull on

1/ This Arab mare has only been ridden a few times. In the round pen, she was stopping okay, but now in the arena, she isn't thinking "stop." As a result, she braced in this sequence when I asked her. I'm trotting her here.

2/ Now, I've asked her to stop by moving my hands back (compare their position to photo 1).

127

3/ She's bracing against the bit.

4/ She is starting to stop, however.

5/ Notice that the position of my hands has not changed. As she pulled on me, I didn't pull harder on her.

6/ Although it has taken several steps for her to stop, I give her slack as a reward.

his face. But that comes with time.

Right now, I'll say whoa, sit down, and lightly pull on the reins. I don't pull hard. I don't care how long he takes to stop as long as he comes to a stop. If it takes 10 strides, that's fine with me. Over a period of time, I will work on making it nine strides, then eight, seven, six, etc.

In the first 30 days, I'm not looking for any kind of abrupt or sliding stop. Even if a colt wants to stop, he's not physically ready to handle it. He needs more riding and conditioning to develop his bones, muscles, tendons, etc., so he can handle faster stops without hurting himself.

After I've been loping a colt around and stop him, I let him stand there and relax for maybe a minute. I've found that a lot of horses won't breathe for the first 3 or 4 seconds after you have stopped them. It's like they are waiting to see what you're going to ask them to do next. I let them stand there, relax, and breathe, so they understand that stopping is a reward. Pretty soon when you've been loping them awhile and you say whoa and sit down, a little trigger goes off in their heads: "I get to stop and breathe!"

It won't be long before you can lope a colt, get him fairly tired, say whoa and sit down, and he'll come to a stop pretty much on his own. Although I don't do this every time I ride a colt, I also try to end the training session by loping him, saying

1/ Here's another sequence of the Arab mare—taken after I had stopped her a few more times.

2/ I'm asking her to stop. I'm out of position here because I like to ride with a lot of slack in my reins. But I'm still pulling easy.

3/ She came to a stop in a much shorter distance, and did not brace against the bit.

4/ After stopping this time, I asked her to take a few steps back. This helps get her hindquarters under her, and helps soften her mouth. She is yielding to the bit nicely.

whoa and letting him stop, and then getting off and leading him to the barn. This is the *ultimate* reward.

Then there are colts a little on the lazy side and always looking to stop. If I even cough or hiccup, they stop. With a colt like this, I won't stop him as often because he'll start to scotch (anticipate stopping) all the time. Instead, I'll just ease him down to a walk from the trot or lope. If he does anticipate stopping, I'll encourage him to keep going. I'll do lots of things at the walk and trot without ever stopping; when he needs some air, I'll let him walk for a while.

In working with a colt and teaching him to stop, one thing you should not do is pull hard. A lot of riders figure that the only way to make a horse stop faster is to pull harder. Among other things, this causes the horse to brace his jaw and neck so the pull won't hurt him. So the rider figures, "Well, I didn't pull hard enough." Next time he pulls even harder, and the horse braces even harder.

To make good stops, a horse must be soft and supple in his mouth and body. You achieve that with a light touch. A good game to play with your horse is to see how lightly you can pull on him to get

1/ This is a gelding that has had almost 30 days of riding. He's moving well at the trot.

2/ I've made contact with his mouth and his response time is much faster than the Arab mare. He dropped his hindquarters as soon as I took hold of him.

3/ He's almost stopped. His front legs are still moving—he's not bracing. I'm just sitting, waiting for him to finish stopping.

4/ I give him slack and let him rest for a minute as his reward.

him to do something, whether it's stopping, turning, or backing up. If it takes 5 pounds of pressure to get him to, say, stop, see if you can get it done with only 3 pounds within several days. If you can't, sneak up to 4 pounds, then ease back down to 3, and then 2, and then 1.

If your horse is used to being pulled on, it will take you awhile, because when you say whoa, he's going to brace. When the hard pull doesn't come, he'll be confused at first, and he might not get stopped until he's traveled maybe 25 feet. That's okay. Just sit there a minute, pat him on the neck once or twice, then lope off again.

Again, pick up the reins as lightly as you can when you sit down and say whoa. The horse should stop in a shorter distance. He's starting to catch on: "Hey! If I stop when he says whoa, I get to rest—and he doesn't pull on me!" Eventually your horse will come to a nice stop on just the verbal whoa.

But remember, your horse must be relaxed and quiet for this to work. If he's charged up like a race horse, you won't have any luck.

Backing

Your horse has already been prepared for this from the ground work. Therefore, when you mount up the first few times and ask him to back, he should comprehend and take one or two steps back. That's far enough for the first few rides.

When I back a colt, I apply firm, but light, pressure on the mouth. Severe pressure or jerking will cause him to brace against the bit. He'll probably throw his head up, which "hollows out" his back, making it more difficult for him to pick up his feet to move them back.

When a horse backs properly, he gives to the pressure of the bit, flexes at the poll, and rounds (or arches) his back.

Although I don't use the verbal command *back,* some people do and I don't see anything wrong with it if it helps you out. Nor do I use much body English, such as leaning back. I might tilt back just a little the first few rides to help the colt comprehend what I want. But after that I depend on the reins and my legs.

I consider my legs the gas pedal—to ask the horse to move, whether it's going forward or backing up. On a very green colt, however, I can't use much leg because he doesn't understand leg pressure. So I have to gradually build to it over a period of time. During the second or third week of riding him, I'll pick up the reins and start him backing, them bump him once or twice with my legs to encourage him to take a few more steps back.

When I ask a colt to back, I take as light a hold as possible. But it's not a steady pull with equal pressure from both my hands. That makes it easier for the colt to brace against the pull by leaning on the bit. Instead, I alternate the pressure, but it's not a see-saw motion; i.e., pulling with one hand, then the other. I use my fingers to create a vibrating motion, first from one hand very briefly, then the other.

That makes it uncomfortable for him to lean on the bit; because he's already been taught to back away from pressure on the bit, he should take a step back. Instantly I drop the reins as his reward. Even if he just sort of leans back, I'll reward him. That tells him that yes, moving back is the way to go. If I waited until he took a full step, he might get confused and move into the pressure. That will just make my job more difficult.

1/ This sequence shows the colt backing. At this point he is backing reluctantly. He is giving to the rein and flexing more than he is moving his feet.

2/ To get him to move better, I bump him with my feet.

131

3/ When I bumped him, he could not go forward because he would run into the bit . . . so he began backing more freely.

The sooner you can recognize a very small response in a horse, and reward it, the faster he'll learn and the better you can train him.

If your colt just plain refuses to back up, repeat some of your ground lessons. Back him on a lead rope; and then back him while driving him. Or, while you are mounted and are asking him to back, have an assistant stand beside him and encourage him to back. Sometimes that's all it takes to get a colt untracked and moving back with a rider on him.

If I have a horse that's a little tough to back, I don't take a solid hold of him with both hands. As I've already said, that just makes it easy for him to brace against the pull.

Instead, I'll pull harder on one rein than the other. Let's say it's the right rein. I keep pulling on the right rein, while keeping just enough steady pressure on the left rein so he doesn't turn around to the right. I don't want him to turn; I want him to back off the right rein. As soon as he quits leaning on the right rein, I release the pressure. When he's soft on the right side, I'll work on the left side.

It's really very simple. If he's not leaning on the left rein, and he's not leaning on the right rein, then—*voila!*—you've got it. Simply take the slack out of both reins and ask him to back real easy. As soon as he takes a step back, I give him slack as a reward. I now have a starting place to build from.

Logging, Slickers, Etc.

When I'm riding a colt, I'm continually sacking him out by getting him used to different things. For example, riding him through brush, up and down dirt banks, through water, around trees. This seems elementary, I know, but some of these things can be scary to a colt raised in a pen or stall and who has never been outside of an arena. It's a whole new world to him. He's especially wary of crossing water, partly because he doesn't know how deep it is. To his way of thinking, he could be stepping into a bottomless hole. And if it's making noise, like a rushing creek, it seems even more dangerous.

Riding my colts outside gets them introduced to a lot of new things. If you don't have any place outside of an arena to ride, set up some obstacles in your arena. Not obstacles that require a high skill level, such as in a trail horse class, but simple things, like several logs or railroad ties. Just walking over them introduces him to something new, and breaks up the monotony of training. Later you can trot and lope over them.

One thing I like to do with all my colts is get them used to my handling a rope, and to the feel of the rope brushing against their legs or coming across their rumps. Some of the colts I break might never be roped on, but at least they will be familiar with a rope. It helps them learn to accept new things quietly and confidently, because they know they will not be hurt.

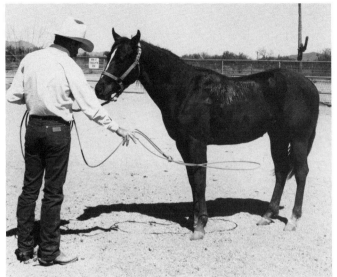 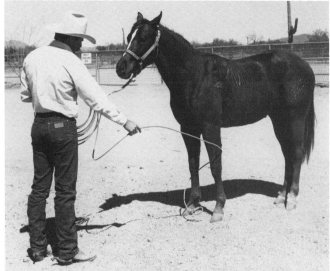

Any horse should be accustomed to the feel of a rope around his legs, and the four pictures on this page show one way to do it. Some riders like to do this while they are mounted and that's okay. In fact, I do it that way. But if you have a colt still too young to ride, you can start on the ground like this.

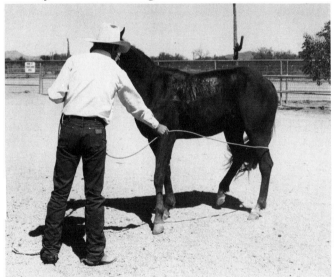 

Some of the colts I break might never be roped on, but at least they will be familiar with a rope.

1/ This set of pictures shows how you can accustom a colt to a rope when you are mounted. I suggest that you start by swinging the end of it.

2/ Next, let it drag against his hip. For safety's sake, do not tie the rope to the saddle horn. Hold the coils in your left hand, as shown, and be ready to drop the entire rope if it should spook the colt.

3/ After dragging the rope, I'm turning the colt around so he can see it.

4/ It startled him, and he started backing away from it.

5/ After he settled down, I flipped it back and forth over his head.

6/ I'm deliberately letting it get around his back legs. I'll do the same with the front legs.

1/ Once a colt is used to the rope, I like to drag a log. I keep an old rope tied to a log in my arena, and here, I'm reaching for the rope.

2/ I flip the rope so the colt can see that it's hooked on to something.

3/ I ask the colt to back up so he can feel the weight of the log. I've got the rope dallied around the saddle horn.

4/ Then I turn him and begin dragging the log across the arena.

I also like to drag a railroad tie on my colts. It's not real heavy so that it puts too much strain on a colt, but it's heavy enough that he knows something is dragging behind him. The weight and the feel of the rope bouncing on his rump add to his all-around education.

So does learning to stand quietly while I put on a slicker. I get him used to it first while I'm on the ground. I sort of flop it around him so he can see it, then toss it over the saddle, as well as over his neck and rump—any place he might feel it flop on him when the rider puts it on. Later I'll mount and do the same thing.

How fast I proceed with some of these things depends on the individual colt. If a colt is nervous, I take lots of time, and do not introduce anything new until he has totally relaxed and accepted whatever I've done up to that point.

For him to quietly accept everything I ask him to do, he must have total confidence that nothing is going to hurt him. The first time I pull a log on him, he might turn and look at it several times, but then he will drop his head and walk off. He thinks, "Well, everything we've done up to now has been all right, so this must be okay, too."

I have most of the colts I break for 90 days or less. There is no way I can introduce them to everything they might encounter in a lifetime in this amount of time. That's why it's so important to teach each colt that no matter what his rider does, he should accept it and relax because he realizes it's not going to hurt him.

136

5/ When I turn the colt so he's facing the log again, he starts backing to get away from it.

6/ Because the log keeps following him, he thinks it is chasing him, and he backs even faster.

7/ To take the pressure off the colt and let him relax, I turn the rope loose. These pictures illustrate why you should never tie the rope hard-and-fast to the saddle horn.

8/ After he settles down, I pick up the rope and back him a few more times until he is no longer afraid of the log.

How Long To Ride a Colt

People frequently ask me how long I ride a colt each day, and I don't have a standard answer. Some colts need more riding than others, and it also depends on what you do with a colt. You can ride him a lot longer on a quiet trail ride than you can if you are drilling him on maneuvers in the arena.

I like my colts to work, though. I like 'em to work. I like 'em to sweat. There's nothing wrong with sweat. If this colt is going to be used, he's got to learn to work, so he needs conditioning.

What is bad, however, is overworking him, which will discourage him from trying, and asking him to do things that put too much physical stress on him. Things like fast stops, roll-backs, spins, and hard galloping. Most colts are broke as 2-year-olds these days, and we tend to

forget that, although they might be big in size, their bones, ligaments, tendons, and bodies are far from mature. They are more susceptible to injury than are older horses.

The mind of a 2-year-old, as well as a 3-year-old, is also immature. If you keep drilling a colt, he gets mentally tired as well as physically tired. When he finds he gets no relief, then he will quit trying. He might go through the motions, but his heart isn't in it. Mentally, he has tuned you out.

To be more specific, an hour is a good length of time to ride a 2-year-old. But you shouldn't be training the entire hour. When I get on a colt, I spend a little time walking him, then trotting to let him warm up. Horses are athletes and they need to warm up—stretch their muscles and limber up—especially if they have been in a stall.

What I do after the colt has warmed up

137

1/ It's good to slicker-break every horse, and I do it with all of the colts I start. Here, I'm letting the colt sniff the slicker.

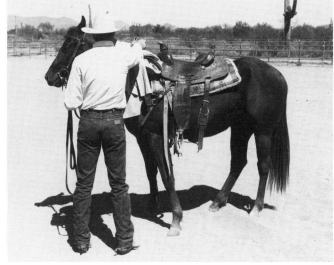

2/ I lay it across his neck, then slide it back and forth, and up and down his neck.

3/ Rubbing it across his hip.

4/ Unfolding the slicker and letting it slide down his hip.

5/ I repeat everything on the right side that I did on the left side.

6/ Letting the entire slicker lie across his neck.

7/ Once he no longer shows any fear of the slicker, I mount.

8/ I rub it up and down his neck . . .

9/ . . . and down his hips.

10/ Now it's time to slip it on.

11/ Before I ask him to walk off, I let him get used to the feel of the slicker on his hindquarters.

12/ Riding off.

depends on the particular colt and how far along he is in his training. I might work on some suppling exercises, especially if he is stiff somewhere, like in circling to the left. I might do some easy stops, and side-pass or two-track him a little to improve his response to leg pressure. Whatever he needs, I'll work on, but I keep it varied to make it more interesting to him.

But I don't go-go-go the entire hour. I'll let him stand and relax after I stop him. If a friend comes by, I'll sit on the colt while I visit. After 30 minutes in the arena, I might ride him out in the desert. Or I might ride him in the desert first, then in the arena. Out of the whole hour, I might train on him only 20 minutes. Or maybe only 10 minutes if he's being real good and trying hard.

The more a horse tries, the better I'm going to treat him. If he's been doing super for the past few days, I just might ride him out in the desert, quietly walking, trotting, and loping. I'd rather do that instead of riding him 10 minutes and putting him up, because then I'm not keeping him in condition. Colts need to be ridden regularly to keep them fit; what's bad is training on them constantly the entire time you're on them.

I believe colts need to be ridden at least 5 days a week, if not 6. Most trainers take 1 day off, and the horses need at least 1 day off, too. If you keep your colt in a stall or pen, he could be turned out on his day off or on days when you can't ride. Then the next day when you get on, he won't be high and silly because he's so full of energy. It's also a good idea to cut back on the horse's grain ration on days when he's not ridden. That will help keep him from getting too fresh, and will lessen the chance of his tying up when you get back on him.

When I am through riding a colt, he usually is sweaty, especially here in Arizona. So unless it's too chilly on a winter day, I rinse the colt off with a garden hose. That makes him feel better and lessens the time I have to spend currying and brushing him. When you do this, be sure to rinse him thoroughly between his back legs—an area that gets real sweaty, but is sometimes overlooked by a rider or groom.

1/ In this sequence, I'm asking the colt to step across the log in the arena. He's extremely leery of it, however, especially since he thought it had been chasing him a few minutes earlier.

2/ After I walk the colt up to it, he tries to escape to his left . . .

141

3/ . . . and then to his right. Because this colt responds to leg pressure, I am able to keep him facing the log. Having him in a snaffle, so I can use direct reining, is also a big help. The combination of leg pressure and direct reining gives me the control to prevent him from whirling away.

4/ Finally he stops to look at it.

6/ From the other side, the log looks different, and the colt approaches cautiously.

5/ After a few minutes of my encouraging him, and blocking his attempted escapes to both the right and left, he rushes across the log.

7/ *Finally he steps over, after a few half-hearted attempts to escape to the left and right.*

8/ *After he crosses the log several more times, in both directions, he relaxes and walks up to it . . .*

9/ *. . . and steps over quietly.*

13 DEVELOPING THE MOUTH

When I take a light hold of his mouth, I want to feel his jaw soften and give.

WHY: Continuing to teach the colt how to respond properly to the bit.

HOW: Careful use of the hands.

PROBLEMS: Asking for too much too soon; being rough; not being firm enough.

WHEN WE first bridled our colt, we began developing his mouth. Through ground work, driving, and first rides, we have already given him the fundamentals to become a soft-mouthed horse. Now it's just a matter of continuing what we have started.

When I take a light hold of his mouth, I want to feel his jaw soften and give. The lighter I can get him to respond, the better. In doing this, the feel is so important. If you are not experienced in doing this, you have to concentrate so that when you feel the jaw soften ever so slightly, you instantly release the pressure. He doesn't have to "bridle up" like a show horse the first day, or even in the first 2 months. All you are trying to do is teach him to drop his nose and give to the pressure.

When I'm doing this, I don't actually

1/ In this sequence, I'm just starting to take up the slack in the reins, asking the filly to give to the bit.

2/ I've made contact with her mouth, and she is just starting to soften.

3/ She drops off the bit nicely . . .

pull. I alternate the pressure in my hands and fingers in taking the slack out of the reins. I alternate doing this with both reins simultaneously, and doing it with one rein at a time. I'll do the latter especially if the colt is stiff in giving me his head when he's moving either right or left. Say it's to the right. While I'm walking him in a circle, I'll take the slack out of the right rein, just enough so I can feel his mouth. As soon as I feel him give his head to me, I'll give the rein back to him.

I'm teaching him that he's not going to be able to take his head back until he gives in and softens to me. The instant he does, I give it back to him.

I'll follow the same principle when I ask him to flex vertically. If a colt learns this from day one, he'll be a lot easier to teach. But if he's gotten away with rooting his nose out, or sticking it up in the air, you'll have to undo this bad habit first.

Some riders who have no feel or finesse in their hands can't tell when the colt, or horse, softens to the pull. So they keep a steady pull, or pull even harder. What happens? The colt throws his head up in the air to get relief, and the rider, either intentionally or unintentionally, gives him slack. Or the rider might try to hang on to the reins a time or two, but then figures the method isn't working, so he quits. The colt has now learned that in order to get relief, he has to stick his nose in the air.

I like to think that I am as smart as my

4/ . . . and I give her slack as a reward.

saddle. When I bit this colt up and tie the reins to the saddle, the saddle holds the colt's head consistently steady while he moves around the pen. The colt doesn't root at the bit, or try to toss his head. If he

Because of the way their necks are built, some horses can flex more easily than others. George's horse is a good example. He's got some length to his neck, the neck is longer on the top line than the bottom, and it's fairly clean around the throatlatch. When George puts pressure on the reins (bottom photo), the horse can easily flex in response. A short, thick-necked horse would have trouble.

does try, the saddle instantly tells him no, and bumps his mouth. So the colt continues holding his head right where it ought to be.

The problem with so many people is that they try to be smarter than their saddles. They think their timing is better than that of their saddles, but it's not. So don't try to be smarter than your saddle. Keep very steady hands. When the colt pulls on

you, just hold your hands steady like the saddle would. Let the colt keep pulling until he figures out that he can't get away with it. Then when he gives you his nose, give him instant relief.

The only adjustment I would make—from my saddle doing it to my hands doing it—is this: I would hold more firmly on whichever side the colt is pulling harder. You will find that most colts (and horses) are less responsive on one side of the mouth than the other. It's easier for a colt to lean on a bit when there is equal pressure on both bars of his mouth. By pulling harder on one rein, I take that advantage away from him, and make it more difficult for him to lean on the bit.

Suppose I put 5 pounds of pressure on both reins; that's 2½ pounds of pressure on each side of his mouth. But if I pull on only one rein, then he gets the full 5 pounds on that side of his mouth, and is much more likely to yield to that pressure and give me his head.

After I have softened one side of his mouth, I work on the other. Over a period of time, I reduce the amount of pressure on the reins—until I can simply wiggle one rein or the other and the horse promptly responds to it. Then I go back to asking him to flex vertically—at the walk, trot, and lope.

Initially, give the colt relief as soon as you feel his jaw soften. But as he becomes more responsive, ask him to hold his head in the vertical position for a longer period of time. For example, ask him to hold his head vertical for two strides. When he can do this comfortably for several days in a row, ask him to hold it for three strides, then four, etc.

You eventually want to be able to put this colt's head anywhere you want it: up, down, and to both sides. If you have problems, go back to the round pen and bit him up . . . using a ring snaffle. I don't like to move a colt into a curb bit until he responds softly and lightly to the snaffle at all three gaits.

Once in a great while you'll have a colt that overflexes. Then the rider must be careful to use exceptionally light hands. Sometimes it will be necessary to use a thick rubber snaffle, which has a milder action than a regular steel snaffle.

This colt is farther along in his training than the filly shown on the first pages of this chapter. Here, he's trotting and I maintain his forward motion while asking him to come off the bit.

There was more of a feel than a noticeable change of head position. But as I felt him soften, I still gave him slack as his reward. As I repeat this over a period of time, he will begin to give more quickly and more noticeably.

Again, I'm asking the colt to continue moving forward while I take a light hold of his mouth.

As he softened his mouth, I softened my hands and gave him slack. This time you can see a more noticeable change.

14 30 TO 90 DAYS

I am going to ask him to be a little bit better at everything I have started him on.

WHAT: An accelerated version of the first 30 days.

WHY: Improving the basics that he learned in the first 30 days.

HOW: Building on what he has already learned.

PROBLEMS: Pushing him too fast.

I CONSIDER the 30 to 90 days that I ride a colt to be an accelerated version of what I have done in the first 30 days. I am going to ask him to be a little bit better at every-thing I have started him on. Before going further, however, I want to point out that how fast a colt progresses depends on the individual colt.

Just because some colts are doing things at 30 days doesn't mean all colts will be doing them. If your colt can't yet do some of the simple things, he won't be able to do the harder things. So don't rush him. Stay slow, stay consistent, and let the colt learn at his own speed. Don't arbitrarily decide that since you have now ridden this

I continue building a foundation on a colt by riding him outside as much as I can. Here, I'm using my inside (right) leg to help this colt develop an arc in his body. Riding him around the bush is a big help. If you can't ride outside, you can do the same thing in an arena, using a barrel.

1/ *This sequence shows how I steady the front end while moving the hindquarters to the left in a turn on the forehand. I am steadying her head with the reins while I bump her with my right leg.*

2/ *While her front end remains stationary, she's crossing over behind.*

colt 30 days, you should begin teaching him more advanced maneuvers.

Don't forget, either, that your colt's lack of progress can possibly be a reflection of your lack of training skills. This isn't a bad thing. After all, no one was born a skilled trainer; we've all had to learn. Just don't blame your colt if he seems a little slow at picking some things up. Instead, try to improve your means of asking him, to make him better understand what you want.

Also keep in mind that your colt can have a problem, such as poor eyesight, a lack of agility, stiffness in turning one way or the other, or a psychological quirk, such as being very timid or very bold. You might be thinking that he's just plain stupid, when he actually has a problem that, if it's identified and overcome, will enable him to be a much better student. Always observe your horse and try to determine *why* he is doing what he is doing.

Also remember that not every horse has what it takes to be a world champion. Be realistic about your horse's abilities and train him to his own level of ability. Don't try to make him something that he isn't. For example, suppose you want a barrel horse, but your colt doesn't have the speed, ability, or desire. He wants to do nothing more than walk, jog, and lope quietly. Settle for this, or sell the colt to

3/ *The mare has responded well, considering that she's just learning this. Because she is so green, I won't ask her to go any farther. Instead, I'll let her rest a minute, then ask her to turn on her forehand the other way.*

149

1/ If a colt, or even a broke horse, starts cutting corners in the arena, here's one way to correct the problem. Here, I am traveling to the left. As I approach the end of the arena, I head the mare straight to the fence.

2/ She's still trying to go to her left as we reach the fence.

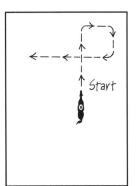

This diagram illustrates the drill I'm doing in the photos on this page.

3/ I stop her just long enough to turn her to the right.

4/ I then leg her back into a trot, complete a circle to the right, and continue traveling around the arena to the left. If you practice this drill at every corner, a horse soon stops cutting the corners because he expects to be turned the opposite direction.

someone who will appreciate a good pleasure horse, and you go look for another barrel prospect.

During the first 30 days, we have put a good foundation on our colt. From this start, we will keep building—a process that continues, or should continue, all of the horse's life until he is finally retired to pasture. At this stage, we have a nice colt who goes along and does whatever we ask in a willing manner. He may not be perfect yet, but he has the idea of what we want. We simply continue practicing regularly so he can get better at it.

Walk, Trot, Lope

During the first 30 days, a colt might not walk out like he should, tending to laze along; or he might be a little nervous and keep breaking into a trot. By now he should be more relaxed, walking out on a loose rein.

He should be able to extend his trot without breaking into the lope. When I extend the trot, I stand in my stirrups and let the colt travel somewhere—outside across the desert. When I want to ease him to a slower trot, I sit down in the saddle. He should continue at a nice, easy trot without slowing to a walk.

Your colt should be able to trot balanced circles, both large and small, to the right and to the left. I will trot a lot of figure eights on a loose rein.

He should also be able to lope consistently true circles, not ones that are egg-shaped or that wander all over. Put a perfect circle in your mind and follow it. The horse must also lope circles without veering off to one side or shouldering out. Some horses do this on the side of the circle closest to the gate or barn.

When a horse wants to do this, I'll use my outside leg and rein to hold him in. Or, I'll cut the circle short; I'll ask him to turn before he's expecting it, and then use my outside leg and rein to keep him from drifting toward the gate.

Leg Pressure

Once the colt is consistent at moving away from my legs, I will go on to the next step: controlling the front end and hindquarters separately. This gives me greater control when I start teaching more advanced maneuvers.

1/ This colt has been ridden about 30 days and is stopping well from the lope. He's moving at a pretty good lope here.

2/ When I ask him to stop, he starts to drop his hindquarters, while his front feet keep moving instead of bracing. When a horse braces, he stops on his front end, giving you that bounce-bounce-bounce. If I can keep his front end moving like this whenever I ask him to stop, he will learn to drive better with his hindquarters. This is necessary to get his rear end under him to make progressively better stops—and ultimately, the long, sliding stops typical of good reining horses.

1/ This colt has been ridden long enough that he's starting to get the basics of a good turn-around. While walking him in a circle, I stop him and ask him to take a big step to the inside—to his left.

2/ He's got his pivot foot (left hind) planted and is taking a big step to the inside.

It doesn't matter which end you work on first, but I'll first describe the turn on the forehand in which the front end remains stationary while the hindquarters move in a circle around the front end.

I use the reins to steady his front end while I move the hindquarters with my leg. To move the hindquarters to the left, I bump him with my right leg and steady his head with the reins. As soon as he takes a step or two in the desired direction, I release my leg as his reward. If he tries to move his front end to the left, I hold him with my reins by pulling a little to the right.

When the colt is consistent at taking a few steps with his hind feet, in both directions while his front feet remain stationary, I'll do the same thing while he's walking. What I want is something like a two-track, although it is not as refined as the two-track that dressage people do. If we are walking to the north, for example, I'll move his hindquarters a little to one side with my leg. He's still walking north, but his back feet are tracking a little to one side. Later, I'll do the same thing at a trot.

This is a good, lateral flexing exercise that is accomplished with time. When I ask the horse to move his hindquarters, I slide my leg back about 12 inches to apply pressure. But when I want to move the front end, I use my leg at the cinch. As the colt learns these maneuvers, I do not have to move my leg back; I can apply pressure where it naturally hangs to move either the front end or back end.

In the turn on the haunches, the horse's hindquarters remain stationary while his front end turns. I talked about how to start this in chapter 12, under "Turning." If I want the horse to turn to the right, I apply pressure with my left leg—and with my right leg when going to the left. I "lead" the horse with the inside rein, and also apply light pressure with the indirect rein (neck rein).

Initially, I only ask for a few steps, but with time, the horse should be able to make a complete turn in both directions.

By having control of the horse's head, front end, rib cage, and hindquarters, I can put him into any position I want. This will help me to make him a better horse, and overcome any problems he might start to develop.

Stopping

I never work on stopping at the beginning of a ride. Then, the colt is feeling good and is probably thinking of *going*, not *stopping*. So I work on other things that require this impulsion. When the colt gets a little tired and wants to stop, that's when I ask.

I ask him easy with my hands, say whoa, and let him slow down and stop. He does not have to make an abrupt stop. Even if he only slows to a walk, I'll let him rest at the walk for a few minutes, then trot or lope off some distance, and repeat the process. His reward is getting to rest at the stop, or walk. I am putting him in a position to want the same thing I want. Then when I give him the cue to stop, I let him do what he wants to do: stop. Through repetition, he learns that this cue means to stop. I have then created a learned response.

When this learned response is reinforced enough by repetition, he will respond to the cue even when he is not tired. If this learned response is not abused, and you continue to reinforce it through repetition, the colt will become very consistent.

With an average colt, I can practice this technique three or four times at the end of a ride and have a very consistent stop by the end of a week. Once I have this, I have something to build on.

If you practice this technique consistently, most colts will begin to improve stopping on their own.

One thing I never want a colt to do is lean, brace, or push on the bit. Although I haven't mentioned it until now, it is my No. 1 rule when I'm doing anything with a horse. From the day I first start working with a colt, I never let him do this.

If a horse that is brought to me is stiff, or will brace on the bit, I get him over those problems before I go on with him. The solution is not to pull harder, as that will only make him worse. The answer might lie in bitting him up, especially if he's never been taught to relax and flex.

3/ Although he still has his pivot foot planted, he's not crossing over in front with his outside (right) leg. With more time, he will.

4/ He's reached well to the inside to almost complete a full turn.

**Any horse
should cross a
stream willingly
and quietly.**

1/ In my part of Arizona, there are not many streams, but I like to get my colts water-broke. Any horse should cross a stream willingly and quietly. This colt has probably never seen "live" water and is a little leery of it. I give him time to check it out.

2/ As he tries to escape to his right, I use my right leg and the reins to keep him facing the water.

Another method: If the horse leans on the bit while I'm riding him, I will get him off balance by pulling on only one rein. It's much more difficult for a horse to lean on one side of the bit. It's not only more uncomfortable, it will also unbalance him. When he comes off the bit, I reward him with slack. I always work on the "heaviest" side of his mouth so I can lighten it up. Doing this consistently will gradually get him over the habit of leaning on the bit.

Right- or Left-Handed

At this stage, if you see your horse is going better one way than the other, take a look at your program and make sure you are giving his "bad" side adequate attention. It's true that horses can be right- or left-handed. But by working them both ways from the start, they should stay fairly even.

If you notice the horse can do things better on one side, or goes better in one direction, spend more time on the bad side. I always work a colt on his weakest areas; if I don't, it's going to hold him back and cause problems elsewhere.

3/ I urge him forward with my legs.

4/ He takes a tentative step into the water . . .

5/ . . . and splashes right in when he realizes there's nothing to fear.

15   LOADING

With all the horse shows, rodeos, jackpot ropings, trail rides, and other events being held, you sure want a horse that you can load into the trailer and head down the road.

WHAT: Teaching to load in a trailer, wash rack, or swimming pool.

WHY: So you can haul him, and easily lead him anywhere else you want him to go.

HOW: Teach him to move away from pressure; do it a little at a time; don't try to pull him in because you can't.

PROBLEMS: Trying to force the horse in; not taking the time to teach him properly; using a trailer that's too small for him, too dark inside, or is too high off the ground; poor driving.

EVERY HORSE ought to know how to load willingly into a trailer and ride quietly. If a horse won't, it can diminish his value considerably, and restrict how much you can use him. With all the horse shows, rodeos, jackpot ropings, trail rides, and other events being held, you sure want a horse that you can load into the trailer and head down the road.

Like everything else we teach our colts, we should set aside a specific time for teaching them to load. Waiting until you *have* to load a colt, or horse, to go somewhere is the worst possible time you can

Before I ask this mare to load, I first position her alongside a fence and teach her to move forward when I cluck. I'll cluck, then tap with the whip if she doesn't respond.

After she learns to move forward, I teach her to back—so I can back her out of the trailer.

do it. Then you are in a hurry, your patience is short, the colt is confused, you lose your temper, and you get in a fight with the colt. He may get hurt, you may get hurt, and even if you succeed in getting him in, he will be frightened and might not haul well. Next time you go to load him, he'll be just as frightened, and it will take you even longer to get him in. From then on, you might have a fight every time you want to load him.

If you'll take extra time to load a colt or horse the first time and do it properly, and then load him every day for a week, you will save yourself years of frustration. You should consider trailer-loading part of his education, just like sacking out and driving.

The method I use in loading is the same technique I use in teaching a reluctant horse to walk into a set of stocks, a wash rack, or a swimming pool. Some of the horse farms here in the Scottsdale area have equine swimming pools. One farm, a couple of years ago, had a bunch of horses they wanted to swim every day, but were having a terrible time getting them into the water. They were trying to rush them, were not having any luck at all, and got several hurt.

They called and asked if I could help,

This is a trailer I frequently use for teaching colts to load. It is braced so it will not roll, and so the front end will not tip up when the colt steps in.

157

1/ This is an Arabian mare, about 9 years old, that has never been loaded. She is a broodmare on the farm where she was foaled. I've led her up to the trailer and am rubbing her forehead to reassure her that everything's okay.

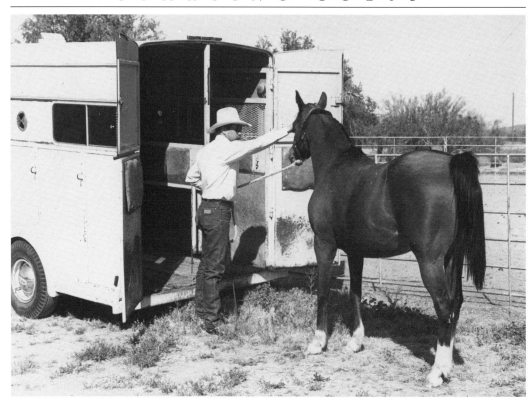

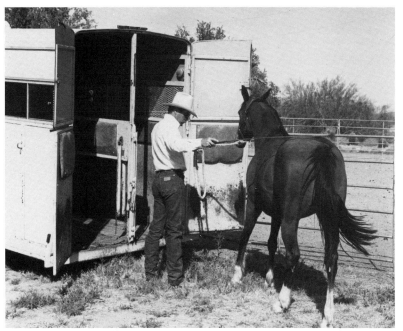

2/ I've clucked, asking her to step forward; she did not respond, so I'm tapping her with the whip.

and on the first day I put 20 head into the water. It took a little time, but on the second day, they all went right in—and then I put another 20 in. I "loaded" them into the pool with the same method I use for loading into a trailer.

Too many people rely on using force to load a horse. But nobody is physically strong enough to drag a horse into the trailer. Instead, the horse needs to learn

to get in because you ask him to. Before explaining how I do this, I want to talk about trailers first.

It helps to look at your trailer from the horse's perspective. The standard two-horse trailer can be a little spooky to a horse, especially if it's dark inside because it might not have windows, or has a dark interior paint job. It can also be too small for him, and make him feel claustrophobic. You'll always hear people say, "Yeah, but I've hauled a bigger horse than him in that trailer." That doesn't mean the other horse wasn't too big for the trailer. It probably means that he was good-minded and easy to get along with.

With a colt, or any horse that hasn't been loaded, it's better to use a good-size trailer for his lessons. Once he has learned to load and is accustomed to being inside the trailer, then you can usually haul him in anything. But start with something big and roomy.

A stock trailer is ideal for horses. It's large, so they have plenty of room, and you can usually lead them in. Sometimes it's the only answer for horses that are not good haulers . . . the ones that scramble by leaning one way and trying to climb up the opposite wall, or the ones that paw and kick a lot. A stock trailer is also good for teaching a horse to load, but sooner or later you will probably have to teach him to load in a standard two-horse.

Use a good trailer, and have it hooked up to your truck, or towing vehicle. You don't want to chance the trailer rolling, or the front end tipping up when the horse steps in. That can scare him, especially when it slams back down and hits the ground.

If you are working by yourself, park the trailer so you have a wing on one side. I usually work from the left side of the horse, so I park the trailer with a fence along the right side. Also park it on safe footing. Grass, asphalt, and concrete are too dangerous because the horse can easily slip and fall.

If you can manage to park the trailer so the wheels are in a depression in the ground, that's all the better because it puts the trailer floor lower to the ground. This makes it easier for the horse to step in—and back out. Once he has learned, then it's no problem for him to step up or down. But for now, make it as easy as you can for him.

The method I use is to teach the horse to move forward, while I'm standing beside him, when I cluck to him. I start this before I get the horse anywhere close to the trailer. I'll position him with a fence on his right side, and have a whip in my right hand. I'll cluck to him, then tap him on his rear end, asking him to take astep forward.

Once in a while, I'll have a horse that starts backing up. The answer is to keep tapping until he finally takes a step forward. Then I immediately stop to let him know he did the right thing. If I stopped while he was backing up, he'd think that's what he's supposed to do.

After about 20 or 30 seconds, I cluck to him again; if he doesn't move, I begin tapping him once more. When I say tapping, that's exactly what I mean—a tap, tap, tap. I am not hurting him, just bothering him enough to make him want it to stop, which he learns will happen when he steps forward.

It won't take long until the horse starts moving forward as soon as I cluck to him, and hold my arm up in the air as if I were going to tap him. Eventually I won't even have to hold the whip; I can just cluck and he will walk forward.

After the horse learns to move forward readily when I cluck, I'll spend some time backing him. This is often neglected in

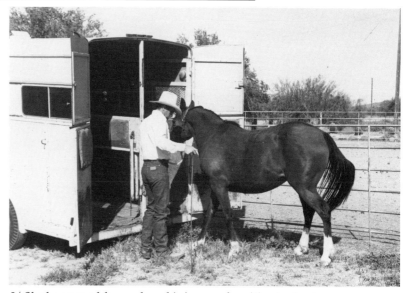

3/ *She has moved forward, and is in a good position to step in.*

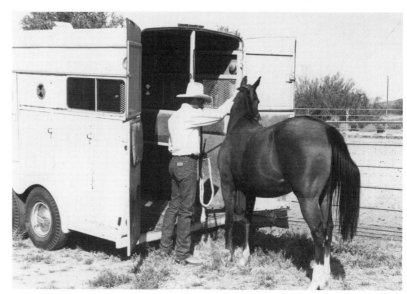

4/ *I pet her and let her relax for a minute.*

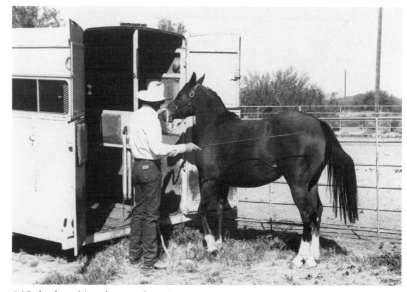

5/ *I cluck, asking for another step.*

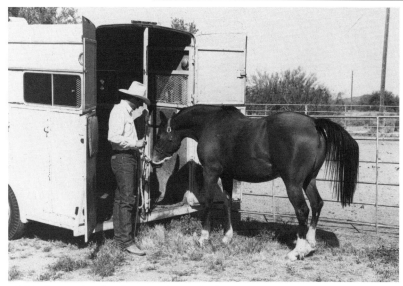

6/ She lowers her head to get a better look.

7/ Now I back her away to take the pressure off of her, and to let her relax a minute.

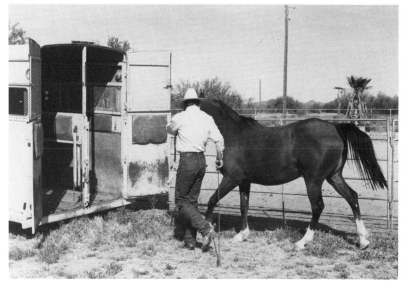

8/ I lead her forward again.

trailer-loading lessons. More than one person has gotten into trouble after loading a colt the first time, but then can't get him out because the colt doesn't respond to a tug backwards on the halter. Refer to the chapter on leading, as it also covers backing.

If the colt, or horse, is nervous during these lessons, go real slow and easy with him, and tap him very lightly—just enough to make him move.

Not until the horse has learned to lead and back is he ready to load. If it's a horse that I don't expect any trouble with, I'll use a regular lead rope on him. If it's a horse I expect trouble with, like a wild horse that I'm breaking, I'll use a long catch rope on him, and run it up through the ring in the manger and back to my hand.

If the horse is at all nervous about being next to the trailer, I'll just let him stand there a little while, rubbing him and maybe putting a little hay on the floor of the trailer. I won't ask him to load until he has settled down. Trying to rush him in would be the worst thing I could do; he would become even more upset, and lose confidence in me.

I'll do the same thing I did before: cluck to ask him to move, and if he doesn't, begin tapping with the whip. Each time he takes a step toward the trailer, I'll stop, maybe pat him; and then cluck again.

It's important to keep the horse's head pointed toward the trailer. But, do not pull on the rope to encourage him to walk in; that is why you are tapping him from behind. Pulling on his head when he doesn't want to lead will cause him to start fighting the lead rope. I only use the rope to give him the direction; clucking and tapping will make him take a step forward.

He might try to swing his hindquarters to the right, but the fence will stop him. It's not as likely that he'll come to the left because I'm standing there. But if he does, the rope coming back to my hand should discourage him. If necessary, I can even tap him on his left side to move him over.

When the horse is right up to the trailer, I'll let him drop his head and sniff the floor if he wants to. I'm not going to hurry him. When he seems satisfied that everything's okay, I'll resume the procedure: cluck, then tap, if necessary.

Sometimes when a horse first puts one

foot into the trailer, he'll sort of paw a few times, trying to get an idea of how solid the floor is. That's okay. But then I'll start again and ask him to put the other foot in. When he does, I'll let him relax and look around inside. But if he starts backing out, I'll resume tapping immediately and will not stop until he stops backing.

Then I'll let him relax a minute before asking him to move farther in. Or, if I see that the horse is really nervous, I might back him out, let him relax, and start over. Or I might quit for that day. I don't think it creates a problem to not get him all the way in during the first lesson. After all, if he has done everything I asked up to that point, why not reward him by backing him out and putting him up. When I bring him back to the trailer the next day, he'll think "this is no big deal," and will be a lot more relaxed.

To me, this is like getting on a colt the first day you work with him. You might be able to, but that doesn't mean you have to. Go slowly. Work at a pace your horse is comfortable with.

When the horse has both front feet in the trailer, it's important not to get impatient and start hurrying him. If you rush him now, you might startle or upset him and undo everything you have accomplished so far. His reaction will usually be to back out as fast as he can because he's afraid he'll be trapped inside. I cannot emphasize enough how critical it is to *go slowly*.

When a horse does start pulling back, it's usually because the handler is putting too much pressure on him. Often it's because he gets impatient after a few minutes and gives the horse a good whack . . . and the horse starts to run back. That's why it's good to have a long rope on him. Once you get him stopped, and you get him up to the trailer again, remember why he started pulling back, and go slower and easier.

When the horse finally picks up one back foot to step in, he'll usually follow with the other—and you've got him all the way in. When this happens, most horses will step up to the manger, but a few will try to run back out. So be ready, and start tapping him on the butt as soon as he starts backing up.

If he does back all the way out, however, don't reprimand him. Let him stand quietly a few minutes, then ask him to

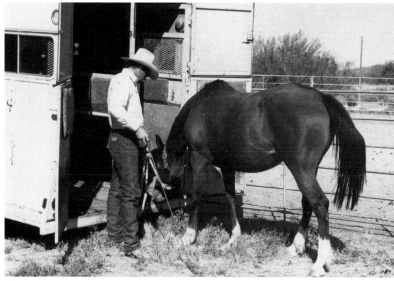

9/ She's checking it out, taking an even closer look.

10/ After I stepped into the trailer, I clucked—asking her to step forward. She didn't, so I tapped her with the whip and this time she responded.

reload. He will soon realize that once he's in the trailer, there's nothing to fear, and he will relax and stay there.

Normally I'm not in favor of giving treats to a horse everytime he does a little trick for me. However, when loading him in the trailer, I want him to think it's a nice place to be, so I will have hay in the manger, or even a little grain, as a reward.

But, I will not use the old stick-and-carrot trick—holding a carrot, or can of grain, or flake of hay in front of the horse's nose to coax him in. That is not consistent with what I am teaching him, which is to get into the trailer because I have asked him to. To coax him in with a treat is to beg him to get in. And I would probably have to do it every time I wanted to load him. He'd soon figure out

11/ *She's halfway in.*

12/ *Once again, I back her out to take the pressure off and to make sure I can back her out once she is all the way in.*

he could buffalo me; if I don't give him a treat, he doesn't have to go in.

Usually when I'm training a horse to load, I do it every day about noon time. He will be hungry, and will look forward to getting in the trailer for his snack. I'll let him stay in there 10 or 15 minutes. After several days of this, he will load easily because he thinks it's a good deal.

I want him to learn that when I lead him up to the trailer and give him the cue to go forward and walk in, he walks in. Once he has loaded, then he can have a reward.

If a horse is really spooked by the trailer, you can park the trailer in the corral and let him eat in it. Do this before you ever ask him to load. Brace the trailer so it won't tip or roll, or even leave it hooked to your truck, with the trailer inside the corral gate and the truck outside so the horse can't damage it.

At first, put the hay just inside the trailer, on the floor, so the horse can easily reach it. Every day, push the hay in a little farther. He will get to where he likes eating out of the trailer and will walk up to it very easily. Then move the hay all the way forward so the horse actually has to step in with his front end. Finally, put the hay in the manger, so the horse has to go all the way in.

Some people have asked if they could follow this method with water, instead of hay, but I don't think that's a good idea. Water is too important to a horse, and he should never be deprived of it.

Another thing you can do to familiarize a horse with the trailer is tie him to it every day for 15 or 20 minutes. You can even tie him at the back end so he can look inside. But always have the trailer hooked up. You can have an awful wreck if a trailer starts rolling with a horse tied to it.

Once a horse has lost his fear of the trailer, he'll be a lot easier to load. Remember this if you lead a horse up to the trailer for his first lesson and you see that he's scared to death of it. Back off, and spend several more days in preparation. Don't think that just because you've led him up to it, you've got to finish the lesson. Rome wasn't built in one day.

If a horse is consistently afraid of a trailer, it could be because something bad happens to him every time he gets close to it, or in it. And very likely it's because he expects a fight and a whipping to force him in. You never want the horse to relate the trailer to something bad happening; that's why we want to teach the horse easily and quietly, and give him a reward once he has loaded.

Older Horses

Some older horses are problem loaders. They have learned they don't have to get into the trailer, because their owners or handlers lack the experience to get them loaded. Or, they might put up a fight every time before they reluctantly get in. These horses can be more difficult to train to load willingly because they immediately get defensive when they are led up to a trailer.

On the other hand, some older horses load quickly as soon as they figure out they can't buffalo their handlers anymore.

With any older horse, I use the same method that I do with colts. It just might take a little longer. My loading theory is always to encourage the horse by tapping him from behind, and not by pulling on his head. As I've said, there's no way you can pull a horse into a trailer.

With an older horse that develops a loading problem, it's a good idea to try to figure out why. If it's a horse that's hauled a lot, he might be tired of it. Horses can get tired of going down the road, just like people do. Take a look at your trailer and see if something is bothering him. Maybe it rattles. Maybe it doesn't have enough ventilation and he gets too hot, especially if you keep a blanket on him. If it's an enclosed trailer, body heat from the horse(s) can raise the temperature inside considerably, even on a cold day.

Maybe he's outgrown the trailer and feels like a sardine stuffed into a can. Maybe he can't raise his head high enough to be comfortable. If he can't see out, maybe he'd be happier in a trailer with windows. Any of these things can make him reluctant to load.

I once had a mare that I sold to some customers. She'd load in the trailer and ride just fine. After about a year, they called and told me she was getting tough to load, and would kick when the trailer was going down the road. It turned out that she was just plain trailer-sour. Every weekend she was hauled somewhere and shown in six or eight classes. It was go, go, go all the time.

13/ If this mare had been upset or really nervous about the trailer, I would have quit for the day at this point. Then when I brought her back the next day, she would be far more relaxed.

14/ This mare was not uptight, so after letting her relax a minute, I ask her to step in again.

15/ She steps in.

163

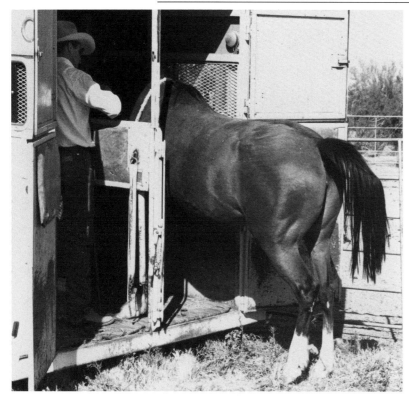

16/ I let her relax and look around inside the trailer.

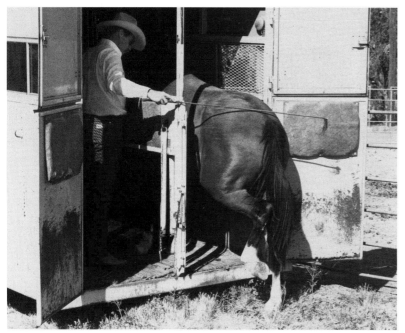

17/ I ask her to move her back feet in.

They laid her off about 60 days, and the problem was solved. She would step right into the trailer and ride beautifully. After that, the owners were careful to give her more R & R.

Driving Habits

Some horses are subjected to such awful driving that you can't blame them for not wanting to get into the trailer. If you have never ridden in your trailer, you ought to. You'll find it doesn't ride nearly as nicely as your truck or car. Most people accelerate once they get the truck turned around a corner, forgetting that the trailer is still turning, and as a result the horse is snapped around—just like in a game that kids play called crack the whip. Jackrabbit starts and stops also contribute to the problem.

Poor driving usually causes a horse to start "scrambling" in the trailer, whereby he leans to one side and tries to climb up the opposite side. Or he will paw, kick, and generally fret. If your horse starts doing this, it's a darn good bet that your driving is causing it. The solution is simple: SLOW DOWN.

A lot of people ask me if they should tie a horse in the trailer, and I always say that it depends on the horse. With an older horse that's used to being hauled, there is no reason to tie him—unless he's a stud being hauled with a mare or gelding. A horse that's not tied will ride just fine, and you don't have to worry about untying him before you take down the butt bar. At one time or another everybody has forgotten to do this. The horse just gets his back feet on the ground when he realizes he's still tied, and he either lunges back in, or rears back trying to break loose. Either way, he can get hurt.

With a young horse, or small horse, it is usually a good idea to tie him. Otherwise he could get his head down between his front legs, or turned back to the side, and not be able to straighten out.

A lot of people use those trailer ties that have a panic snap on one end, and they are okay. But some of them are too short and will cause a horse to panic. He'll take a step or two back, find his head tied, then lunge forward, often into the manger.

The rule of thumb: The tie should be long enough so the horse hits the butt bar before he hits the end of the tie.

164

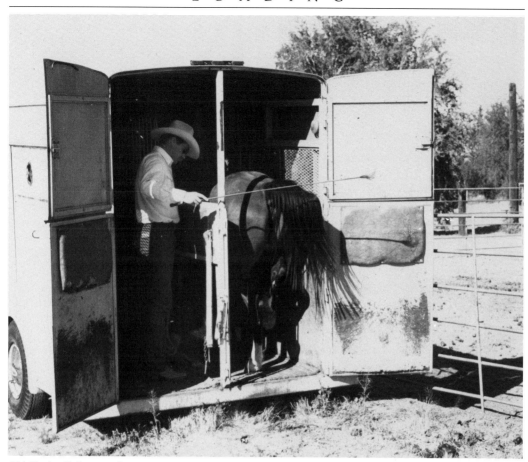

18/ She's all the way in.

Some horses are subjected to such awful driving that you can't blame them for not wanting to get into the trailer.

19/ I pat her, and let her enjoy a little bit of grain in the manger as her reward.

Although Mike is best known for his talents in breaking colts, he can turn out reining, cutting, and other finished horses.

A native Arizonan, Mike Kevil was born in 1953 in Glendale, a Phoenix suburb. His dad, George Edward Kevil, a Thunderbird pilot in the United States Air Force, was killed in a flying accident when Mike was 2 years old. His mother, Georgia, married Walter Ruesga when Mike was 7, and later the family moved to California, where he attended high school.

Mike has one brother, George, and four sisters: Penny Dibrito, Georgia Surina, Annette Taylor, and Terri Hollingsworth. He and George have helped each other out and worked together since they were kids. Mike and George both competed in rodeo in high school, with bull riding being their main event. "My brother was always better at it than me; he was a good bullfighter, too," says Mike. George went on to compete in collegiate rodeo for Pierce College and in the R.C.A. before it became the PRCA.

Mike describes his own college career as " . . . very brief. I had a scholarship to Mount San Antonio College in Walnut, Calif., and I stayed there for a semester and a half. But I was having more fun out of school than in, so I quit and went to Colorado."

Although Mike regrets not staying in college for a formal education, his travels gave him an education of a different sort, plus a wide range of skills. "I've learned something from everyone I've met and in every place I've been."

In Estes Park, Colo., Mike worked for Keith Hagler at Sombrero Stables, which runs hundreds of horses that are leased to packers, outfitters, and dude stables. Working with so many horses of various breeding, ability, disposition, and temperament was an invaluable experience for Mike.

"Keith Hagler believed in learning by doing. The first pack trip I went on, I was the guide. I told Keith I didn't even know where I was going, much less how to pack or cook. He told me not to worry about it and spent a whole 10 minutes educating me on the subject." That's 10 minutes more instruction than Mike had when he first drove a semi-truck for Keith. "We were going down the freeway. Keith climbed out of the driver's seat and said, 'Come on over!'"

From Colorado, Mike went to Idaho where he trained and rode horses for Kenny Kimble, a race trainer who also ran a dude stable.

Mike returned to Arizona to look for a job ". . . doing anything. I was flat broke. One day a friend told me about a guy who needed a horse broke. I guess he thought I did an all right job because

Don Dodge has sent many colts to Mike for starting.

he recommended me to his neighbor. Pretty soon I was riding three horses at $5.00 a head, every day. It was the first time in a couple of months I'd been able to feed myself! I thought it was a pretty good way to make a living, so I put an ad in the paper to get more horses." Before long, Mike had to cancel the ad. He had more horses than he could ride. "I kept my saddle in my pickup all the time. I didn't have a place of my own, so I made house calls. I broke horses in back yards, barbed-wire arenas, open desert, plowed fields . . . whatever was available."

In the winter of 1976, Mike went to work for Gene LaCroix at Lasma Arabians in Scottsdale. "I started an awful lot of colts for Gene. I was there for a while, and then I went to work for Shorty Freeman. After that I went to Texas to ride for Matlock Rose." When asked about working for such outstanding trainers, Mike says, "I never had a game plan. Good opportunities kept coming up and I just took them."

When Mike returned to Arizona, he went into business for himself. Don Dodge, Al Dunning, and other trainers started sending him colts to break. Because of his long association with Al and the number of colts he was riding for him, Mike put up his own barn at Al's stable in Scottsdale. After 2 years there, he was able to buy his own facility north of Scottsdale, near Cave Creek.

Mike (right) with his sister, Penny Dibrito, and brother, George.

Mike rides lots of horses for individual owners, but 50 percent of his business comes from other trainers who send him colts to break and problem horses to fix. The types of horses that Mike rides cover the spectrum. It's not unusual for him to step off an Arabian park horse, then onto a rope horse to heel a few steers. He has broke a number of BLM mustangs for their adoptive owners, and each year gives clinics for mustang and other horse associations.

He has also given clinics at several state prisons where mustangs are gentled in a federal program designed to be mutually beneficial to both horses and inmates. On two occasions Mike has flown to Italy, where he has given clinics and helped his Italian hosts with their horses at home and in the show ring. He was interviewed by several magazines there, and has had his own articles published in Italian horse magazines.

Mike's interests vary as much as the horses he rides. He is continually educating himself and starting new projects. When asked about the future he says, "Who knows? All these opportunities keep coming up and I'd like to give them all a shot."

—Pat Close

Mike (mounted) and George working a heifer.

The *Western Horseman*, established in 1936, is the world's leading horse publication.
For subscription information: 800-877-5278. To order other *Western Horseman* books: 800-874-6774.
Western Horseman, Box 7980, Colorado Springs, CO 80933-7980. Web-site: www.westernhorseman.com.

Books Published by Western Horseman Inc.

ARABIAN LEGENDS by Marian K. Carpenter
280 pages and 319 photographs. Abu Farwa, *Aladdinn, *Ansata
Ibn Halima, *Bask, Bay-Abi, Bay El Bey, Bint Sahara, Fadjur,
Ferzon, Indraff, Khemosabi, *Morafic, *Muscat, *Naborr, *Padron,
*Raffles, *Raseyn, *Sakr, Samtyr, *Sanacht, *Serafix, Skorage,
*Witez II, Xenophonn.

BACON & BEANS by Stella Hughes
144 pages and 200-plus recipes for delicious western chow.

BARREL RACING by Sharon Camarillo
144 pages and 200 photographs. Tells how to train and compete
successfully.

CALF ROPING by Roy Cooper
144 pages and 280 photographs covering roping and tying.

CUTTING by Leon Harrel
144 pages and 200 photographs. Complete guide on this popular sport.

FIRST HORSE by Fran Devereux Smith
176 pages, 160 black-and-white photos, about 40 illustrations. Step-by-
step information for the first-time horse owner and/or novice rider.

HEALTH PROBLEMS by Robert M. Miller, D.V.M.
144 pages on management, illness and injuries, lameness, mares and
foals, and more.

HORSEMAN'S SCRAPBOOK by Randy Steffen
144 pages and 250 illustrations. A collection of handy hints.

IMPRINT TRAINING by Robert M. Miller, D.V.M.
144 pages and 250 photographs. Learn to "program" newborn foals.

LEGENDS by Diane C. Simmons
168 pages and 214 photographs. Barbra B, Bert, Chicaro Bill,
Cowboy P-12, Depth Charge (TB), Doc Bar, Go Man Go, Hard Twist,
Hollywood Gold, Joe Hancock, Joe Reed P-3, Joe Reed II, King
P-234, King Fritz, Leo, Peppy, Plaudit, Poco Bueno, Poco Tivio,
Queenie, Quick M Silver, Shue Fly, Star Duster, Three Bars (TB), Top
Deck (TB), and Wimpy P-1.

LEGENDS 2 by Jim Goodhue, Frank Holmes, Phil
Livingston, Diane C. Simmons
192 pages and 224 photographs. Clabber, Driftwood, Easy Jet,
Grey Badger II, Jessie James, Jet Deck, Joe Bailey P-4 (Gonzales), Joe
Bailey (Weatherford), King's Pistol, Lena's Bar, Lightning Bar, Lucky
Blanton, Midnight, Midnight Jr, Moon Deck, My Texas Dandy, Okla-
homa Star, Oklahoma Star Jr., Peter McCue, Rocket Bar (TB), Skipper W,
Sugar Bars, and Traveler.

LEGENDS 3 by Jim Goodhue, Frank Holmes, Diane Ciarloni,
Kim Guenther, Larry Thornton, Betsy Lynch
208 pages and 196 photographs. Flying Bob, Hollywood Jac 86,
Jackstraw (TB), Maddon's Bright Eyes, Mr Gun Smoke, Old Sorrel,
Piggin String (TB), Poco Lena, Poco Pine, Poco Dell, Question Mark,
Quo Vadis, Royal King, Showdown, Steel Dust, and Two Eyed Jack.

LEGENDS 4
Several authors chronicle the great Quarter Horses Zantanon, Ed Echols,
Zan Parr Bar, Blondy's Dude, Diamonds Sparkle, Woven Web/Miss
Princess, Miss Bank, Rebel Cause, Tonto Bars Hank, Harlan, Lady Bug's
Moon, Dash For Cash, Vandy, Impressive, Fillinic, Zippo Pine Bar, and
Doc O' Lena.

PROBLEM-SOLVING by Marty Marten
248 pages and over 250 photos and illustrations. How to develop a
willing partnership between horse and human to handle trailer-
loading, hard-to-catch, barn-sour, spooking, water-crossing,
herd-bound, and pull-back problems.

NATURAL HORSE-MAN-SHIP by Pat Parelli
224 pages and 275 photographs. Parelli's six keys to a natural horse-
human relationship.

REINING, Completely Revised by Al Dunning
216 pages and over 300 photographs showing how to train horses
for this exciting event.

ROOFS AND RAILS by Gavin Ehringer
144 pages, 128 black-and-white photographs plus drawings, charts,
and floor plans. How to plan and build your ideal horse facility.

STARTING COLTS by Mike Kevil
168 pages and 400 photographs. Step-by-step process in
starting colts.

THE HANK WIESCAMP STORY by Frank Holmes
208 pages and over 260 photographs. The biography of the
legendary breeder of Quarter Horses, Appaloosas, and Paints.

TEAM PENNING by Phil Livingston
144 pages and 200 photographs. How to compete in this popular family sport.

TEAM ROPING WITH JAKE AND CLAY
by Fran Devereux Smith
224 pages and over 200 photographs and illustrations. Learn about
fast times from champions Jake Barnes and Clay O'Brien Cooper.
Solid information about handling a rope, roping dummies, and
heading and heeling for practice and in competition. Also sound
advice about rope horses, roping steers, gear, and horsemanship.

WELL-SHOD by Don Baskins
160 pages, 300 black-and-white photos and illustrations. A horse-
shoeing guide for owners and farriers. The easy-to-read text, illustrations, and photos show step-by-step how to trim and shoe a
horse for a variety of uses. Special attention is paid to corrective
shoeing techniques for horses with various foot and leg problems.

WESTERN HORSEMANSHIP by Richard Shrake
144 pages and 150 photographs. Complete guide to riding western horses.

WESTERN TRAINING by Jack Brainard
With Peter Phinny. 136 pages. Stresses the foundation for western training.

WIN WITH BOB AVILA by Juli S. Thorson
This 128-page, hardbound, full-color book discusses traits that
separate horse-world achievers from also-rans. World champion
horseman Bob Avila shares his philosophies on succeeding as a
competitor, breeder, and trainer.